Global Investing
MADE EASY

Global Investing
MADE EASY

Your wealth-creating guide
to the international markets

Warren Ingram

Global Investing Made Easy
Published by Penguin Books
an imprint of Penguin Random House (Pty) Ltd
Company Reg. No. 1953/000441/07
The Estuaries No. 4, Oxbow Crescent, Century Avenue, Century City, Cape Town, 7441
www.penguinrandomhouse.co.za

First published 2021

1 3 5 7 9 10 8 6 4 2

Publication © Zebra Press 2021
Text © Warren Ingram 2021

Cover image © Vecteezy

All rights reserved. No part of this publication may be reproduced, stored in a retrieval system or transmitted, in any form or by any means, electronic, mechanical, photocopying, recording or otherwise, without the prior written permission of the copyright owners.

PUBLISHER: Marlene Fryer
MANAGING EDITOR: Ronel Richter-Herbert
EDITOR: Christa Büttner-Rohwer
PROOFREADER: Dane Wallace
COVER DESIGN: Sean Robertson
TYPESETTER: Natascha Olivier

Set in 11 pt on 16.5 pt Crimson Pro Regular

Printed by **novus print**, a division of Novus Holdings

978 1 77609 639 8 (print)
978 1 77609 640 4 (ePub)

CONTENTS

Preface ix
1. What is your dream? 1
2. Create your own vision 7
3. Find your passion! 15
4. Financial freedom 21
5. Investments 101 37
6. Inflation, risk and asset mix 55
7. Investing at home and offshore 71
8. Build your global portfolio 89
9. Two scenarios 95
10. Why buy residential property? 107
11. Overview of investment terms 115
12. Money and relationships 129
13. Investment insights from the rich and famous ... 137
14. Financial blunders to avoid 149
Conclusion 159
Further reading 161
About the author 163

This book is dedicated to all those who seek financial freedom. I believe financial freedom is possible for anybody. I believe that people who are free from financial burdens are better able to have a positive impact on their families, friends and society in general. If we could all make a small difference, life would be much better for everyone; we don't need to profit at the expense of the environment or others in society.

PREFACE

This book, which I wrote during the Covid-19 pandemic, was inspired by watching Donald Trump make terrible decisions in the USA's early handling of the pandemic and the European Parliament's dallying in securing vaccines for the citizens of its member states. While this was happening, the tiny state of Israel started procuring and vaccinating its people at lightning speed. Australia took the decision to lock out the rest of the world to isolate the country from Covid-19. How could we forecast which country would do well and how would the economies of the world endure lockdowns and other trade restrictions? I observed scientists, economists and other prognosticators forecasting the end of the world, while deep thinkers like Bill Gates were heralded as prophets for their earlier predictions that pandemics would become the next big threat to the world. Finally, I also learnt that the global media and all their expert sources had only one word to describe the situation: 'unprecedented'. This has to be the word for 2020!

As someone who has spent more than 25 years advising investors about their money, I found that this situation presented some new and unforeseen challenges – and a load of new opportunities. The first major challenge was to realise that no one had a realistic idea of how the pandemic would affect us in the short term, nor did anyone know what would happen in the long term. As soon as I realised this, I was back on familiar ground, because I understood that we were in the middle of an unpredicted event that would cause human beings to react in a predictable fashion.

Predicting how things will work out is always an entertaining but ultimately not very reliable way to make decisions about how we live, work and invest. We have to realise the future is always unpredictable. The pandemic provided an important lesson for our understanding of investments: when we learn that we cannot predict the future, investing becomes much easier. If we follow some basic principles and focus on a few key issues, we can ignore the noise. A key principle of investment is that investors need to spread their money far and wide when the world around us is uncertain. The more uncertain things are, the more we need to spread our money because unpredicted events will also create unpredicted opportunities. Investing in many different countries and assets will enable us to benefit from opportunities that we could never have predicted. Consider the rise of Zoom during the pandemic; a relatively small business benefited greatly from the unexpected circumstances. What about a tiny, new biotech company that suddenly becomes a household name because it is lucky enough to be working on vaccines when a pandemic strikes? Investing our money in many different countries and industries means we can benefit from unexpected growth and reduce the impact of unexpected losses on our investments.

Very few books focus on global investments. There are many American books on investments, and some are written by investment experts, but most of the popular books are written by motivational speakers looking for content to promote their next series of talks, podcasts or TV shows. This book aims to expose you to the wide world of global investments – a world that may seem risky or dangerous. I hope to show you that global investing helps reduce your risk while ensuring more consistent growth for your money over time. Most investors tend to invest too much money in their home countries and not enough in the rest of the world.

In this book I describe how my thoughts and beliefs about investments evolved over time. As I learnt more about investing, human nature, markets and life in general, I came to realise that while many of my earlier ideas about money management may have been correct, I did not spend enough time focusing on the human being behind the money decisions. It is not enough to explain the theory of efficient markets, compounding, diversification and remaining invested in turbulent times. As investors we also need to understand that each of us thinks about money differently. Understanding the science of money is only half the story; the other half is understanding how we as human beings make decisions. Once we understand ourselves and what drives us to make financial decisions, we can consider the theory of investments and determine the best course of action to suit our needs. That means each of us might have a slightly different approach to investing, and what works for one person might not work well for another.

It is worth remembering that investment markets have been around for centuries. Over time, technology has changed every aspect of life. There is a misconception that all these changes must have a fundamental impact on markets. However, Jesse Livermore, a pioneer of day trading, said it best: 'Wall Street never changes, the pockets change, the suckers change, the stocks change, but Wall Street never changes, because human nature never changes.' Technology accelerated stock market cycles, as information now moves around the world in an instant. However, there has been no change in the basic behaviour of markets: we still have long periods of rising markets followed by irrational exuberance and stock market crashes. Then follows a period of mourning and consolidation before the cycle of rising markets begins all over again.

Uncertainty is a fact of life, and the Covid-19 pandemic has taught us that life can change in a heartbeat. Poor decisions by politicians can have a crippling effect on a country's economy, and this can affect our lives directly. Large countries are not immune from bad politicians, economic crises, pandemics or climate change either. For investors this means starting to think about investment differently. It is important to understand that our investments can live and work in many different countries and industries; our money doesn't have to be bound to one small part of the world. Just because someone works in the UK or Australia doesn't mean they should be investing all their money in those countries. In fact, we should consider investing far from home to ensure that we take advantage of opportunities not available to us in our home country. Global investing is a way of managing unforeseen risks that might have an impact on our own country.

As the world is becoming more integrated, it is also becoming much easier to make informed and reasonably safe investments in foreign markets.

Investors who remain fully invested in their home country are limiting themselves and exposing themselves to risk. Even for those who are not planning to ever live in another place, it still makes sense to send money off to other countries to benefit from their industries, climates, resources and technologies.

If you have read my earlier books, you will notice many common themes in this one, but I hope you will find it evolutionary. For my new readers: my aim is to provide you with an impartial education on investments. I believe that we can reduce our mistakes by understanding more about money and about ourselves. The path to financial freedom is not to find the best investments in the world, but rather to avoid the biggest mistakes, remain consistent, and let our money grow while we sleep and live our lives!

DOLLARS OR POUNDS?

One complication when writing a book about global investments is that of choosing what currency to use, so I would like to clarify my choice from the outset. You might be living in the UAE, the UK, Australia or South Africa, and it would obviously not be sensible to cover every country in every example. I chose to use US dollars as my default currency when discussing investments, case studies and concepts. The USA still has the largest stock market in the world, and its currency is often the default for global portfolios. This doesn't mean that all the investments I refer to will be US-based. For example, if you live in the UK and your global investments are denominated in dollars, you will most likely have money invested in China, Taiwan, South Korea, Germany, Japan and other countries. However, these investments are generally consolidated and priced in one currency, often the US dollar, so that you can monitor and manage them more easily.

CHAPTER 1

WHAT IS YOUR DREAM?

Why should we save and invest our money? After all, any decision to save money means we are sacrificing something. What's the point of putting money away now for some future purpose? Most of us would prefer to go on that island holiday now or buy that new car we want – why should we not enjoy those things sooner rather than later? These are the questions we need to answer every time we decide to save rather than spend. It is important for us to find reasons so compelling and so motivating that we are prepared to sacrifice some short-term pleasure to achieve our goals.

Readers of my previous books have shared their stories of success and difficulties with money with me, and I have found that a common theme is how hard it is to find motivation that is strong enough to stop them spending money now. They find it challenging to be consistently disciplined enough to follow the steps required to achieve their financial goals. Their most frequently asked question is this: Is it possible for 'ordinary' people to build wealth?

I believe that people focus on the wrong issues when it comes to money. Many people want to be rich. They don't really know why; they simply like the idea. Very often their motivation is negative; for example, they use sentiments like 'I hate my boss' or 'my job sucks'. Unfortunately, those are not great motivators for us to make financial sacrifices over the long term. Most human beings need positive motivation to work towards something. This is especially true for money goals. You need to find a positive goal that will inspire and motivate you. For most of us, the ideal money goal is to achieve financial freedom. To me, financial freedom means having enough money that will earn me enough income to cover my costs every month so that I don't need to work to pay my bills.

Financial freedom is possible for anyone. If you keep your expenses low, you won't need a great deal of money in investments to cover your monthly expenses. There is a huge difference between being wealthy and being financially free. To be truly wealthy, you will need to work hard and become successful. And you will need luck. It is this last part that makes it impossible for us all to be wealthy. If we consider the founders of Microsoft, Amazon, Alibaba, Tencent or Facebook, it is clear that they were brilliant people. However, they were also lucky enough to be born at the right time and in the right country – one that was primed for them to launch their businesses. Consider if any of these founders had been born in Myanmar, North Korea or Sudan – would they have been able to achieve the same success?

It is also important to understand that you can be wealthy but not financially free. Consider a family that is worth $5 million. In any country, they would be considered wealthy. However, let's assume that the family spend $500 000 every year to maintain their lifestyle. This means they are spending 10% of their wealth every year. If they don't work to earn extra money, they will be broke within a few years. Now consider another family that is worth only $800 000 and has a yearly spending of $32 000. This means they are only spending 4% of their wealth. This level of spending is sustainable – they won't need to work to pay their bills, because they have achieved financial freedom. It is much easier to build up investments of $800 000 than $5 million. Shouldn't we all aim to control our expenses so that our investment goals are easier to achieve?

Over a career of more than 25 years, I have been advising people about their money, and I have met thousands of individuals who have achieved financial freedom. They come from many different countries, they have different levels of education, and very few of them had inherited money or received a financial education from their parents. While they are all different, I find that they have one thing in common: they do not make excuses or give up on their goals. Their vision is strong enough to keep them going, even in difficult times.

I believe that it is absolutely vital to have a deeper motivation or vision to be a successful saver and investor. If you have a vision for how you want life to be, it helps you make the small sacrifices that are necessary if you want to save every month. Your vision also helps you make smart decisions in difficult times and enables you to remain calm and think clearly when others can't.

This book is not another cheesy motivational book written by a motivational speaker with no history of financial success. This book is aimed at helping you find your own path to financial freedom. A motivational speaker or book cannot inspire you for long periods, because motivation must come from within. This book can help you find a way to keep moving forward when the going gets tough. I have found that it becomes easier to remain motivated once you start tasting success with your savings and investments. Well-known author and inspirational speaker Simon Sinek wrote a great book called *Start with Why*. It has helped me understand why we need a deeper motivation to act. While Sinek's book is aimed at leaders, I believe it is most important to lead ourselves first.

What is your dream?

Most people who have achieved financial freedom had a clear idea of how their lives would be when they reached their goal. They would have been able to show you the place where they wanted to live and the house where they would spend their time, and they would have been able to tell you what they wanted to do with their time.

Your personal vision doesn't have to be grand: you don't need to change the world or send people to Mars. Your goals can be more modest (mine certainly are), but it is important to have your own dream that will motivate you when the going gets tough. For example, on my laptop, I have a picture of a house, a picture of a piece of beautiful countryside, a picture of a sunset from a tropical island and a picture of 15 young people. Those pictures are the first thing I see when I start my laptop, and they all have meaning for me. The house is a design I have created with my wife, and this house will be built on the piece of land in the countryside. I also love travelling to tropical islands and am always planning our next trip. The picture of the 15 young people is meaningful to me because my wife and I have supported them through their schooling and university careers. We have a passion for education, and we aim to help educate as many people as we can. My laptop home screen is my personal vision board, and it keeps me motivated every day. When I get tired or lazy, those pictures remind me of the reasons why I work every day.

If you only live from day to day without a larger plan or vision, you will be much like a boat at sea with no way of steering, no engine, no GPS and no map. You will drift with the current and go where life takes you. This might sound romantic, but if you have a long-term goal, you need to have a map that helps you move towards it.

This map becomes especially important when life knocks you off course and you need to find your way again. It is impossible to figure out where you are if you don't have a map and an idea of where you want to go. This is where your personal vision becomes vitally important. It is the map for your life, and if you work on your map and make it as detailed as possible, you stand the best chance of reaching your goal even if life throws many obstacles in your path.

Why is your personal vision so important?

Approximately 80% of both pre-retirees and recent retirees see their retirement as a new stage of life; it is certainly not an end goal where life stops. Most look forward to the freedom that retirement brings. This is the conclusion of an extensive survey of 9 372 pre-retirees, 2 293 retirees and 451 people who never plan to retire, conducted by Fidelity Investments in collaboration with the Stanford Center on Longevity and Greenwald & Associates in August 2015. 'There seems to be a values shift as people near retirement,' says Stanford University's Steve Vernon. 'Even if they haven't reached their retirement goal in dollar terms, many seem to desire freedom over money.'

If you don't have a vision for your life and something that really motivates you, then the goal of freedom at retirement will not be compelling for you.

We do not really become motivated if we simply try to move away from something, such as a job we hate. Once you are no longer working in a job you hate, what are you going to do? It is very important to work towards a positive and constructive goal – your personal vision. That's how you build a life for yourself.

CHAPTER 2

CREATE YOUR OWN VISION

When you begin to create your own personal vision, try to make it as real and detailed as possible. Can you picture where you want to live? What does your house look like? How often are you going to travel and where do you want to go? What car will you drive? When do you want to be in a position where you no longer need to work for a living? Do you want to continue working once you are financially independent? What else will you do with your time? Do you want to help others, start a charity, or work with distressed animals? These are all examples of the details you should consider when creating your own vision. Everyone's vision will be different, but you need to make yours real and meaningful. The more real it is to you, the easier it will be to make the necessary trade-offs between what you want to do now and how you plan to live in the future.

It starts with time

Time is a factor in any vision, because we have limited time available. That means time must be the anchor in your vision.

I usually suggest to clients that they start with identifying the age at which they would like to achieve their ultimate financial goal. For most people, the ultimate financial goal is financial freedom. This is the stage when you have sufficient money for the income generated by your investments to cover all your expenses, including holidays, travel and vehicles. Many people are approaching financial freedom but have no clear idea what to do with their lives once they have achieved this financial goal. This is why it is important to quantify how you want to spend your time.

When you think about quantifying your time, you need to be realistic. It is not sustainable to spend your time on your favourite sport all day and every day once you have reached your financial goal. You need a clear plan that details how you will spend time on important issues like your health, mental stimulation, family, charity work and travel. As you could live to the age of 85 or 95, this means that you will have nearly half your life to do what you want on your own terms. A plan for your time is as important as a plan for your money!

Clients often ask me how much money they will need to become financially free. As a good rule of thumb, you will need a capital amount of $300 000 for every $1 000 worth of monthly expenses to be sure of living a sustainable life. If you plan to spend $4 000 per month in today's value once you are no longer working, then you will need $1.2 million in capital in today's value to stop working. Depending on where you live or want to live, this number might vary slightly, but it is based on spending 4% of your investment money every year. This is known as the Bengen rule, named after William Bengen, who calculated that this was a safe amount to draw from investments over a long period. In my experience, this is a great guide for investors across the globe. If you have a well-diversified global portfolio, relying on 4% of your investments for income will work in most circumstances.

What do you want your life to be like?

If you have established a clear and defined time for your vision, you have created an anchor for the rest of your vision. Now you can start adding details.

People who don't have a clear game plan for how they will spend their time once they stop working often lead miserable and unhealthy lives. This is why it is important to start clarifying for yourself what you want your life to be like in 20 years' time. You have to decide what is important to you. It is unrealistic to plan to play golf, read or go out for coffee with friends all the time. What are you going to do with your time? Do you still want to continue working, but this time for fun?

After more than 20 years spent advising retirees and pre-retirees, I have come to realise that very few career-orientated people apply sufficient thought to their post-work lives. Specifically, they do not discuss this with their partners. When they eventually stop working and are home all day, their lives take a nasty turn when they find out that their partner has had a life of their own and is not interested in giving it up. The sad part is that this situation could be avoided by having simple conversations about how life should be once both partners are no longer working. It is a mistake to simply assume that both of you have the same goals.

It is worth noting that many high-level executives get divorced in their first year of retirement, and a significant proportion die of illness. According to a survey by Fidelity Investments, more than 60% of husbands who are nearing retirement plan to spend more time with their wives, while only 45% of wives plan to spend more time with their husbands.

We all need positive goals that excite us and inspire us to do more. Only focusing on what you *don't* want to do will not inspire you when you have to make difficult trade-off decisions. If you have a positive vision for your future once you have stopped working, you have a much better chance of living a healthy, successful, enjoyable and fulfilling life. This is especially true if you are married and are working towards a shared vision with your partner.

If you envision yourself being financially independent and want to spend a few months every year travelling, and you also see yourself learning to paint, write books or play a musical instrument, you need to plan for this. If you want to become the next big crime novelist, this is a wonderful goal, especially if you don't need to earn a living doing it. But you still need to develop a plan for this vision, so you might start out in your first year once you have stopped working by enrolling in writing school and doing some writers' retreats before settling down to write your first masterpiece. This is the type of positive planning you need to think about to keep you chipping away at your goals every month while you work towards your vision.

A very sensible way of working towards your vision is by filling out a one-month calendar of how you envision your life once you are financially independent. It is a very practical way of making your vision more concrete.

After all, if you cannot fill your calendar for one month, how will you be spending the next 20 to 40 years of life once you are financially free?

Where do you want to live?

As you work on your personal vision, bear in mind that where you want to live is very important. Where you live will have a huge impact on many other aspects of your vision. Therefore it should be one of the first things you decide. For example, if what excites you is the idea of living in a big city such as New York or London, you will need a very different plan compared to someone who intends to retire in a small town in a rural part of Portugal or stay on in their home town.

It is clear that if you plan on living in a large city, you will need far more capital to have a comfortable life than elsewhere, as it would likely be much more expensive. Someone living in a rural area or small town will be able to live a great life with a lot less capital. So, quite evidently, your desired place of residence will also determine how soon you can achieve financial freedom. A low-cost destination for your future home will mean spending less on accommodation, food, insurance and daily travel. It is also worth your while to spend some time researching where you live at present. Do not simply assume that you will and should continue living in your current home, city or country.

The choice of your future home can always be a part of your initial journey once you have achieved financial freedom. Consider spending some time travelling to various parts of your country of residence and potentially to other parts of the world to determine where you would ultimately like to spend your time. Also, keep in mind that social engagement should play a major role in your decision. As we age – and especially once we stop working – our social network starts to shrink. A strong network of friends and family can contribute hugely towards your happiness and mental wellbeing. When you choose a home for your future, consider how easily you will be able to meet people, communicate with them and develop a strong social network.

Your chosen destination will also shape other aspects of your vision. For instance, if you plan to live far away from family, you may need to plan for more travel and maybe even learn a new language.

As time passes and you move closer to realising your vision, you will find additional motivation by working on more concrete plans for your home. This might include saving money to buy the land you want to live on and to start studying the new language you want to learn. Actions such as these will help to keep you motivated and inspired so that you keep moving towards your goal. Motivation is particularly helpful if you experience a setback – as your vision becomes more real, you become more determined to overcome any problems.

What kind of lifestyle do you want?

This simple question might require significant thought and planning. Some aspects that you will need to consider include the following: Do you like eating at restaurants often? Do you want to engage in an expensive hobby? Do you want to attend live events such as theatre shows or concerts?

Life in a big city means you have access to more restaurants, theatres, museums and other cultural pursuits. If you crave excitement and entertainment, you need to make that part of your vision, so that you can live in a big city. If you are happy with a simple life and like growing your own vegetables, you may want to consider a more rural lifestyle. The cost of life in rural areas is generally lower, which means you need less capital and can work for a shorter period before you can start to live your financially free life.

Some notes on travelling

Many people dream of international travel or of touring around their own country. Alternatively, you might be a real homebody and not enjoy the thought of frantic airports, grumpy immigration officials and being away from your own bed for too long. Because travel is very personal, I believe that travel and holiday plans should form a separate category and be a separate goal from your retirement lifestyle goal.

If you are an avid traveller, holiday planning can motivate you to make financial compromises and avoid unnecessary spending, so that you can accumulate the capital you need to reach your financial freedom goals *and* plan for the holidays you want to take. If you are content with living a simple life at home, you could spend more time and money on travelling.

International travel, especially to tropical islands and going on safari in Africa, is a real motivator for me. It is a core part of my vision for my future life and has helped me to compromise on spending. So I have consistently been saving for travel instead of driving an expensive car. I managed to reach my financial freedom goals at age 45, but I decided to continue working an extra few years so that I will be able to travel more when I retire, and to fly in the bigger seats and stay in better accommodation. This goal has helped me see my work as being less of a hardship and much more fulfilling because I have a clear purpose towards which I work.

A couple I know, who retired with sufficient capital but were not wealthy by any means, decided to sell their large family home and buy a very small home. They then invested the extra money from their large home in a customised off-road camper and towing vehicle. They then spent the biggest part of 15 years of their retirement camping and touring Africa. If they found a place they really enjoyed and that had good weather and offered the company of sociable fellow travellers, they would often spend months in one safari campsite. They set up their entire life so that they never needed to return home unless they chose to do so. In total they spent less than three months of every year at home, and this was usually during school holidays when the roads and national parks got too busy.

Another retiree I know spent a few months every year travelling on cruise ships. He always wanted to travel the world but hated flying and unpacking his bags every few days. Cruising suited him perfectly, and when his wife passed away, he decided to travel. He got to meet new people and make new friends in a comfortable setting that suited him.

I always suggest to my clients that they draw up a 'bucket list' of all the special things they want to do and the places they want to visit during the first few years after they stop working. If you are in a life partnership, be sure to discuss your travel wish list with your partner and agree on the first adventure you want to go on once you have stopped working. This will help to make your vision more concrete.

Do you have a cause?

Some people are terrified by the thought of retirement because they enjoy being busy and want to remain productive and contribute to society for as long as possible. However, if you work for a large corporation, you might not be able to work beyond the age of 65.

Productivity and purpose do not need to be linked to working for a salary. You could dedicate some of your time to a cause that inspires you. For example, if you love animals, you might plan to allocate a portion of every week to an animal shelter. If you have plans to start your own charity or to revitalise an existing one, you might need to allocate capital for your cause. If your cause is meaningful to you, it is worth making it part of your vision.

Creating a stepladder to your vision

Your vision needs to be deeply meaningful to you and real enough to inspire you to work towards making it a reality.

Once you have established your vision, find a way to create a series of small, attainable goals that will serve as measurable milestones for you to reach as you work towards realising your vision. If you only have a grand vision for your life, you will struggle to determine whether you are making progress. Meaningful and measurable progress markers and milestones will help you stay motivated.

Without meaningful and measurable progress, you will lose motivation quickly. Part of the reason for this is that we struggle to visualise ourselves as becoming older. Our older self is a stranger to us, and people struggle to make meaningful sacrifices for strangers. This means that when we have to decide about sacrificing an immediate benefit (such as buying a cheaper vehicle instead of a beautiful but expensive one), we tend to place more value on the immediate benefit of the expensive option because we do not really value our future selves.

Part of the solution to managing this problem is to have a concrete goal, and to break this goal down into a series of smaller steps that we need to follow to attain it. I like to visualise this stepwise approach as a stepladder: our ultimate vision is at the apex of the stepladder, and a series of smaller steps lead from where we are today to the top of the ladder.

> EXAMPLE OF A STEPLADDER TO YOUR VISION
>
> **Final step:** Thirteen years' time: Stop working for an income at age 53. Live in a small rural village with time allocated every day to writing crime novels. Travel for four months every year to tropical islands around the world and to big cities where I can do research for my novels and meet other writers. Ensure that there is sufficient money in my charity to place five needy children in school every year.
>
> **Step 5:** Eleven years' time: Build a home in my chosen rural village.
>
> **Step 4:** Nine years' time: Identify the right rural village and buy the specific piece of land where I want to live.
>
> **Step 3:** Seven years' time: Ensure I have enough capital to buy the land, build my house and live my preferred lifestyle.
>
> **Step 2:** Three years' time: Spend less on replacing my current vehicle so that I can increase my savings.
>
> **Step 1:** Today, when I get to work, I am going to increase the contributions to my retirement funding. The money will come from cancelling unnecessary online subscriptions, which consume my time and add no value to my wellbeing.

CHAPTER 3

FIND YOUR PASSION!

Once you have a vision for your life, this vision will enable you to make some difficult choices about the way you spend your time and money right now. This is especially true in the early days of your saving and investing career, when you need to make sacrifices because your financial resources are likely to be limited. But how you save and invest is only half the story; the other half is what you do to earn an income.

Many people work in careers they hate, for bosses they despise or for companies they don't respect. It probably goes without saying that it is very difficult to be good at a career when you hate the work.

Ideally, you should try to earn your income from doing something you are passionate about. It follows that if you are passionate about your work, you will probably be happy to work hard, and this is the secret to being good at what you do. If you are good at what you do, you are more likely to increase your income, and this will enable you to build up your savings as fast as possible.

It is surprising how few people manage to get this right, and I believe this is partly because they do not find work that they are passionate about. It doesn't matter if you own your business, work for a corporate or work on contract – you need to enjoy your work. Most of us spend more time working than we do with our families and friends. If you do not enjoy your work, it is very likely that you will be unhappy, and this will affect other aspects of your life.

Work is not meant to be 100% fun. If it were fun all the time, it would not be called work. It is not realistic to think you can have a career where you only do what you love – no matter how much the self-help gurus might tell you otherwise. You should be working in a field that interests you and, if possible, be doing something you are passionate about. While you do not have to love your work all of the time to be successful, passion and enjoyment will help a lot.

How to find your passion

I have been to a few Berkshire Hathaway annual general meetings where Warren Buffett and his partner, Charlie Munger, talked about the company, the underlying businesses and how they have fared during the year. Once they were finished talking about their business, they would answer questions posed by analysts, journalists and other members of the audience.

The questions they fielded covered a wide range of topics, from detailed questions about their accounting policies right through to broad issues such as finding your passion in life. Buffett and Munger invested in companies that were managed by people who were absolutely passionate about their businesses.

I remember one young man who asked them how he could find his passion for a career, as he was a student and not passionate about any career. The question stumped Buffett, who said that he had always been passionate about investing. Fortunately, Munger was on hand to provide some sage advice. He said that you should start by excluding those jobs for which you have no talent or natural ability. For example, if you are hoping to be a professional basketball player but you are only 1.5 metres tall, then it probably makes sense to look for a different career. Similarly, if you would like to work at NASA as an aeronautics engineer, but are poor at mathematics, then you should consider a different path for yourself. By a process of elimination, you can narrow down your range of career options until you have a more limited, realistic selection of careers that will suit you. From there, you can select the career that interests you most and provides you with a chance to work to your strengths. This is important, because you will never enjoy something and be properly financially rewarded if you are not good at it.

Even if your aim is to stop working for money and to do something in the field of philanthropy, it is still worth focusing on your career to ensure that you spend your time as wisely as possible and so that you can build up your savings as quickly as possible.

Here are some 'ingredients' of successful careers. One or two may not apply to you, but they are worth bearing in mind as you embark on your career path.

Develop specialist skills

A notable characteristic of successful people is their ability to develop a craft of their own. Most people who have had a long and successful career have developed a certain expertise and set of skills that they have honed over a lifetime.

When you are starting out in your chosen career, do not be afraid to spend the first few years finding what suits you best and then working as hard as possible on building your experience and skills in your chosen field. In other words, the first few years are not necessarily about chasing the maximum income if it means that you are sacrificing the possibility of honing your skills and experience.

In your 20s and early 30s, you should try to get to a position where you are working consistently in one area, so that you can spend the time becoming proficient in your chosen field. Malcolm Gladwell's brilliant book *Outliers* relates many examples of how top musicians, businesspeople and tech superstars spent approximately 10 000 hours becoming experts before they became globally successful.

While you build up your skills and expertise, it is vital that you do your current job brilliantly. It is the only way for others to judge your abilities and hopefully see your potential. Too many people enter the workplace and are so focused on their own potential and ambitions that they find their first jobs demeaning and beneath their abilities. As a result, they do poorly in their 'menial' job, which limits their careers, because their colleagues and managers can only judge them on how they are currently performing. So, work hard and take every task seriously: you never know who is watching and judging you.

Very few generalists are able to retire successfully. A good example is a middle manager in a large corporation – what is that manager's craft? What set of skills does this manager have that makes him or her valuable and unique? People working in large corporations often strive to move into management positions, but is this necessarily a wise ambition? While the fancy titles and potentially higher salaries may seem attractive, you need to realise that a manager holds an essentially generalist position.

My experience of meeting retired people who used to work as high-level managers in large corporates taught me that they seemed dissatisfied with their careers and were relieved that they were no longer in the rat race. Many of them struggled to quantify what they had accomplished after all those years of work.

A better alternative might be to develop the necessary skills and expertise in an area of specialisation that will make you valuable to employers or clients. For example, an experienced engineer is generally more marketable than the general manager who manages an engineering company. Also keep in mind that during times of turmoil, such as when a company goes through mergers or experiences financial difficulties, it is often managers who are let go first.

Do aim to keep a balance, though – there is an equal danger in being a generalist and becoming super-specialised, because you can specialise yourself out of a career. This is particularly true in the tech industry. If you want to specialise, be sure that your skills and experience can be adapted to a changing world.

Be a revenue generator

In bad times, companies very rarely get rid of the people who actually bring in the money. As a revenue generator, you have a high degree of control over your own destiny, and to a large extent your income will be determined by what you can produce for your employer.

Revenue generators are usually in sales – not the career that most parents would wish for their children, as professions such as law and medicine are perceived to be more prestigious. But ironically salespeople often have the better lifestyle, because they don't work 18-hour days and good salespeople tend to earn well.

Leverage yourself – don't sell your time

There are many wealthy people who have made their fortune selling their time. The most obvious examples are lawyers and accountants, but these careers share one drawback: to be successful, these lawyers and accountants have had to sell many, many hours.

The extra hours they sold came at a high cost, because it meant that other parts of their lives suffered. They sacrificed family time, exercise, social activities and outside interests. Often, by the time they retire, they are socially isolated (and often also divorced or never had a life partner) and suffering from poor health. Surely this is not the kind of success anyone in their right minds would wish for themselves?

If you can leverage your time successfully, you have the ability to earn an income even when you are not working, which means you can achieve a balance between work and the other important aspects of your life.

Writers, musicians, actors, podcasters, asset managers, software developers, financial planners and academics are examples of vocations that are not solely driven by selling time. As an example, a lawyer who charges an hourly rate for their work is limited in how much they can earn from clients. You can only work for a fixed number of hours in a day. This means you can increase your rate per hour, but you will not earn money if you are not billing someone.

By contrast, a writer of books or software only needs to write these once. Thereafter the items will be sold, and the writer will earn an income repeatedly from the same piece of writing.

Vision and passion are a powerful combination

I cannot think of a better way to live than doing something I mostly enjoy every day, knowing that I am steadily realising my dreams at the same time.

I also find it amazing how our overall happiness and motivation can improve our ability to handle setbacks more easily. Without a clear road map provided by our vision, and the fuel provided by our passion, we are more likely to drift around letting life and everything around us determine our future. I believe we all want to have the freedom to choose how we spend our time.

CHAPTER 4

FINANCIAL FREEDOM

People are living longer. In the year 1900, the average person could expect to live for 31 years. By 1950, people could expect to live for 48 years, and by 2020 it was 79 years. Some scientists are now telling us that human beings will soon live to age 150. This seems realistic to me, considering that Jeanne Calment lived to be 122, and quite a few people are in line to overtake her record soon. This increase in longevity is making the notion of retirement at age 65 an obsolete concept.

There are a few good reasons to abolish the concept of retirement at age 65. First of all, most of us are much healthier at age 65 than our grandparents were. We are generally able to live very productive and active lives until age 80 and beyond – consider Warren Buffett and Charlie Munger, who ran Berkshire Hathaway when they were already both in their 90s! As the world's population ages more and more, fewer young people are being born, and the world's population is expected to peak around 2064 according to a study published in *The Lancet* in 2020.[1]

That means the world will need people to work longer. There are also good financial reasons for people to continue to work later in life. If we all stopped work at age 65 and then lived to age 110, we would need to fund ourselves for 45 years! The financial mathematics in this scenario do not work, because we would be spending longer living off our money than we spent accumulating it during our careers. So it makes sense to earn an income

---

1 See https://www.thelancet.com/article/S0140-6736(20)30677-2/fulltext.

for longer periods than our parents and grandparents. However, we can change the way we work and exert more control over our lives.

The concept of financial freedom plays an important role in this. If you will be working for 40 to 50 years, it is important that you ensure that your work is enjoyable and that you are not a slave to your salary. Therefore, financial freedom is an important goal: it will help you to have the financial means to make empowered choices about your life.

What is financial freedom?

Complete financial freedom is when the income from your assets exceeds your monthly expenses. The concept of financial freedom differs from being wealthy. It is impossible for everyone to become truly wealthy (despite all the Hollywood fairy tales we consume), but anyone can be financially free.

Some people attain financial freedom with assets under $1 million, while others who have assets of $10 million are still not financially free. I have met many people who retired with relatively small amounts (under $500 000 in investments, and a paid-off home) who are living fantastic lives. The real secret to their success is that they have controlled their expenses and limited their cost of living. If, for example, you only need $3 000 per month to live your life, you will need much less capital to fund this life than someone who needs $10 000 per month. This is such a simple concept, yet very few people take the necessary steps to limit their cost of living so that they may achieve financial freedom sooner. Consider the lawyer who told me that he needs $300 000 per year to fund his lifestyle. I know he has about $3.5 million in investments. That is a lot of money. In most countries, he would be considered wealthy. However, I also know he is not financially free. If he stops working and starts living off his assets, he will only survive for a few years before his assets are eroded. He has the choice of three options: continue working to build more capital, reduce his cost of living, or start playing the lottery in the hopes that he gets lucky one day!

Three simple steps to financial freedom

There are three simple steps to financial freedom:
- **Step 1:** Become debt free.
- **Step 2:** Build an emergency fund.
- **Step 3:** Earn income from your assets to cover your expenses.

STEP 1: *Become debt free*

The crucial step towards financial freedom is to become debt free. Unfortunately, most people struggle to get past this step because they constantly increase their debt burden as their income increases. Many high-income earners are three months away from financial difficulty if they should lose their jobs. They make the mistake of buying a flashier car, a bigger home and more expensive clothes as their income rises. Sadly, they often do this by taking on more debt, as they believe they can carry the higher monthly debt repayments with their bigger salaries. This might seem like a good idea until a financial shock wipes them out – such as the Covid-19 pandemic, which has been a severe example of an unplanned financial shock for many. As your income rises, it would be far more sensible to pay off all your debt and rather fund your lifestyle using cash. I estimate that 80% of income earners are unable to achieve this first step to financial freedom; most people are all too reliant on debt to fund their lifestyle. You can start becoming debt free by setting up a realistic budget that will help you become debt free, and then sticking to it.

STEP 2: *Build an emergency fund*

Once you are debt free, you need to build an emergency fund to protect you from unexpected financial shocks. This is not a form of investment, but rather a way to protect yourself against being forced into debt or other financial difficulties when life happens. People who have an emergency fund are better able to deal with nasty surprises like retrenchment (as has happened to many as a result of Covid-19) or unplanned medical costs. Your emergency fund should be able to cover half your annual expenses, although it could be less if you have other assets that you can access easily, and should be saved in an account you can access quickly and without penalties. Good examples are money market mutual funds, savings accounts at your bank and cash in your investment accounts.

Avoid investing your emergency fund in assets that could lose value, for example direct or indirect investments in stock markets. This is important, because you might need your emergency money in the middle of a big stock market crash, which could mean that your emergency fund has lost half its value when you need it most! Do not expect your emergency fund to grow like the rest of your investments; it has a different job in your financial life. It is like the airbag in a car: you hope that you'll never need it, but you're always glad to know it's there.

STEP 3: *Earn income from your assets to cover your expenses*

The final step to financial freedom is to start building income-generating assets that will eventually pay your lifestyle expenses in the future. This is the step most people focus on – that is, deciding where they should invest their money to get the most growth with the least risk. We'll be looking at various investment options in Chapters 5 and 9.

But there is one implicit aspect that most people ignore about this step: you need to have completed the previous steps before you start investing. I often struggle to convince high-income earners that they must pay off their debts before concerning themselves with investing. They tend to think that this approach is too slow and overly cautious, and that their income and investments will grow so well that they need not concern themselves with debt. While there is some merit in this view, I have seen many people lose their jobs or businesses unexpectedly. So I strongly urge you to limit or pay off your debt first before focusing on investing.

There is one golden rule for managing your money, and it applies to any person at any stage of life and at all levels of wealth: make sure you always spend less than you earn. If you want to be sure that you are saving enough to achieve financial independence and a comfortable retirement, aim to save at least 15% of your total annual income, every year, over your lifetime. The 15% target is not a guarantee for financial freedom, but it is the bare minimum you need to save over your entire working life. It is not good enough to save only later in your career; you need to be disciplined from the start. If you have been working for a few years and have not yet accumulated savings, start now!

It is important to understand that your initial asset base will take the longest to build because the benefit of compounding works in your favour over the longer term. The principle of compounding is most simply explained by an example. In the second example, I show how you can use the principle of compound interest to work out how long it will take to build $1 million.

EXAMPLE 1: THE PRINCIPLE OF COMPOUND INTEREST

When you place $1 000 in an investment, and it grows at 10% per year, you will have an extra $100 at the end of one year. If you leave the growth in the account so that the $1 100 can grow at 10% for another year, you will have an extra $110 at the end of the second year. The reason you earn more in year two is because the extra money from year one is also earning money in year two. If you start with $1 000 and it grows by 10% per year, it will take you about seven years to double your money. If you took the growth out of your account at the end of every year and kept the growth in a separate account, it would take 10 years to double your money. The effect of compounding is really important – it is the real secret to investment success.

EXAMPLE 2: HOW LONG WILL IT TAKE TO BUILD YOUR FIRST $1 MILLION?

Let's say you start an investment account with $10 000. You decide to invest in a global index exchange traded fund (ETF). Every month you add $1 000 to the investment. As your income grows (at 6% per year), you increase your monthly savings at the same rate. After nine years, you will have more than $250 000. After another four years, your money will have doubled to over $500 000. After that, it will take only another four to five years to add a further $500 000 to the investment for it to be worth more than $1 million. In total, in this instance it will take less than 18 years for the investment to grow to $1 million. Of this amount, you will have contributed only about $360 000; the other $640 000 will be compounded growth.

You don't need a million dollars for freedom

My own research indicates that most people can live a good life spending $30 000 per year. If your goal is financial freedom and not being wealthy, I think it is best to plan for a reasonable lifestyle as your main financial goal. If you are planning for an annual lifestyle cost of $30 000, you will need about $750 000 to reach financial freedom. This amount is the value of your investment assets and doesn't include the value of your home or your vehicles.

> WORK OUT YOUR FINANCIAL FREEDOM NUMBER
>
> If you want to work out your financial freedom number, here is my rough guide:
>
> Calculate your monthly expenses (e.g. $2 500) and multiply this amount by 12 to get your annual expense amount. In my example, this will be $30 000. Then multiply this amount by 25 to work out your financial freedom number, which in this example will be $750 000. If you have saved $750 000, I would advise you to invest this money in a global account that owns shares, property, bonds and a bit of cash. If the portfolio is properly balanced, you should be able to take 4% from your investment every year while it continues to grow. The 4% works out to $30 000 per year. Over a typical 10-year period, this investment should grow around 8% to 10% every year, so the amount keeps growing even though you are taking out 4% every year. This means you will be able to draw a bit more every year to pay for the rising lifestyle costs caused by inflation.

The real secret to financial freedom is to ensure that your expenses are as low as possible. Far sooner than you think, this will put you in a position where you do not need to earn a salary to survive. I realise that many people do not want to live on $30 000 a year, but if you can get to this position, you will be able to make better decisions about your life without worrying about a salary. Most people who reach this position can change their lives substantially – for several good reasons:

- You have less stress because you do not have to generate a salary every month.

- You have the freedom to do the work you choose – for example, start a business.
- You can do a job you like rather than a job you hate.
- If you have a lousy boss, you can quit and take time to find a workplace that suits you better.

While I would never suggest that it is easy to become financially free, it is certainly within your reach.

Let's talk about debt

For most people, debt is a weapon of wealth destruction. Financial institutions love to offer you debt, and they make it really easy to spend your debt as fast as possible. This is dangerous because we are seduced into spending money that we don't have on stuff we don't need! Most of the world's savvy investors avoid personal debt at all costs. I know that many famous personal finance personalities recommend using debt to build your wealth, but I believe this is really dangerous advice and an unreliable path to financial freedom. There is a major lesson to learn here: debt kills people – literally. Debt is a major cause of suicide, divorce, stress and unhappiness in relationships. Debt can be a valuable financial tool, but in my view, it should be used only in very rare circumstances. Here are the three most common types of debt:

- Short-term debt (including credit cards and personal loans): This can only be described as bad debt and should be avoided – always.
- Medium-term debt (including loans for vehicles financed over 36 to 72 months): You can use debt to buy a car but be careful and do your homework. Many people spend too much on cars. Try to put down a large deposit on your car, as this will reduce your monthly repayments and help you get better finance terms from the bank.
- Long-term debt (including home loans): This type of debt can be considered good debt, because you are incurring debt to purchase something that could appreciate in value. Most people will take a loan from a bank to buy a home and then aim to pay off that loan over 20 to

30 years. In an ideal scenario, the home will grow in value so that it maintains its worth against inflation. This means that you can sell the home one day and get real value for the asset. However, you should try to ensure that your debt repayments are small enough so that you can pay all the running expenses of the property and still save money.

In other words, there are times when you can make use of debt, but you need to be careful and treat it as a necessary evil rather than a way to live a better lifestyle. If you can't afford to buy nice things without debt, then you can't afford them. Those who live without debt early in their careers are always in a better financial position than those who live with debt.

Is there a time when debt is good for you?

Many people have created their fortunes by using debt to buy growth assets (or productive assets, as I prefer to call them). These are assets that are able to generate an income and have the potential to increase in capital value too. The theory behind good debt is simple: you can, for example, buy a house with debt and then rent it out. Over time, your rent should exceed your debt-repayment costs and so the property eventually pays for itself. But if you are tempted to use debt to create wealth, it is important to understand the nature of the asset you are buying and the certainty of your income before making such a major decision.

Let's look more closely at the example of buying a house. If you had bought a house with a 100% mortgage at the peak of the property market in 2008, you might have got yourself into major financial difficulties in the global financial crisis, when house prices collapsed in the USA. This caused a knock-on collapse in many countries around the world. Rental income for most properties stagnated or declined from 2008 to 2012 as large numbers of people lost their jobs. If you were relying on rent and your own income to pay for the property, you would have been in deep trouble if both you and your tenants had lost your jobs. This happened to thousands of people around the world in 2008.

This scenario shows that you should be very careful when using debt to build your wealth. Start by determining whether the asset you want to buy is really a productive asset. Productive assets are those whose capital value is likely to increase at a faster rate than inflation. In addition, these assets might also generate a regular income.

Farmland, for example, is a productive asset because it should appreciate in value and will produce goods that can be sold regularly. Other types of productive assets include commercial property and business ownership. Government bonds can be productive assets if they generate an inflation-beating income. By contrast, I am not convinced that money market investments (cash) are productive assets, because your interest rate is unlikely to exceed the inflation rate in the long term.

Once you have decided on an appropriate productive asset, it is important not to take on too much debt to purchase it. You need to be sure that you will be able to repay the debt in all circumstances. For example, if interest rates rise by 2% from current rates, will you be able to fund the debt? If you become unemployed, will the income from the asset be sufficient to cover the debt repayments? If not, do you have sufficient cash reserves to fund the shortfall until you get another job?

I am highlighting these points because they can derail your best-laid plans. This doesn't mean you should avoid debt when buying productive assets; you merely need to exercise caution. Many wealthy people have created their fortunes using some debt. For example, some academics argue that Warren Buffett built his multinational investment company, Berkshire Hathaway, into a multibillion-dollar business through gearing.

Use of gearing

Gearing is usually indicated as a percentage and shows how much debt a company has as a percentage of its assets (called equity). If a company has assets worth $100 000 and debt worth $60 000, then its gearing is 60%. It could be argued that Buffett used money that his company did not actually own – i.e. debt – to buy quality investments.

To illustrate, when he bought shares in Coca-Cola, he might have bought $160 million worth of shares, but as Berkshire actually only had $100 million, the balance was borrowed. As the dividends from Coca-Cola were paid to Buffett's company, he used them to pay the financing costs on the $60 million.

Over time, the $160 million increased in value substantially and made the original debt seem minuscule in comparison to the new value of the shares. People who are successful in building their wealth with debt can exercise good judgement with the purchases they make and the level of debt they take on to fund the purchases.

I believe the optimal level of debt on productive assets for any person is 15% to 50% of that person's assets. This means that if you have $1 million in assets, you should borrow a maximum of $500 000 to buy additional productive assets. No doubt some people would argue that you could take on more debt to generate better growth more quickly, but I believe you cannot rush wealth creation. If you want to become wealthy in a short time, you will need to marry someone rich, become a corrupt politician or rely on luck. If you want to take a calculated risk with a high probability of success, be conservative with your debt and be patient.

Planning: The key to wealth

It is worth saying this again, in case you don't already know: the earlier you start saving, the better for your long-term wealth. But there are also enormous advantages to planning how you save and spend your money.

A report by UBS Wealth Management in Switzerland highlights the difference in wealth between people who are good planners versus those who are bad planners. It shows that if you do not budget or have investment and retirement plans, you are guaranteeing that you will limit your wealth over your lifetime. The report also shows that even a small amount of planning can make a massive difference.

Budgeting

There's no avoiding it: you need to budget. Too many people get to the week before payday wondering where their money went. By the time they get to retirement age, they will be wondering why they have no real savings.

If you find yourself in this position on a monthly basis, it is almost certain that you don't have a budget. There are a range of useful online budgeting tools should you need help in setting up and managing a budget. These allow you to itemise and categorise your monthly costs automatically by allowing the tool to access your banking information.

A good budget can be very simple but, more importantly, it should be realistic. Do not start with what you should spend. Rather start with what you actually spend. For example, if you are currently spending $3 000 per month on food, restaurants and entertainment, there is little point in budgeting an amount of only $2 000 from next month onwards. Rather start by reducing your budgeted expenses by $30 a month and see if you can stick to it. This will help you to progressively decrease your costs over time to a level that is realistic, and that doesn't reduce you to the life of a home-bound hermit. This principle should apply to all your variable expenses (costs that vary from month to month), as some expenses, such as your rent or mortgage, are not variable (these costs stay the same over time).

In addition, start budgeting to save some money every month. Try to save a minimum of 15% of your gross salary every month. In other words, if you earn $300 000 per year, then you need to save at least $45 000 per year. If this seems to be too high, start with a smaller amount like $3 000 per month and then progressively increase your savings over time as your income increases. The saving target of 15% is the minimum that you should aim to save over your lifetime, although it would be better to save more so that you can be sure of living the life you want when you stop working one day. The best savers save $33 out of every $100 they earn!

Planning your savings and investments

There is a simple principle at play when it comes to saving and investing: the more you plan your finances, the greater your chances of being wealthy.

Your plans do not need to be complicated. If you start with a simple budget and stick to it, you will eventually get to the point where you are building up savings. You can use these savings to build your cash safety net. Once your emergency fund is established, you can start your investment planning.

Like your budget, your investment plan can be very simple. It could simply be a monthly investment into an ETF or shares or mutual funds. If you don't want to manage your investments on your own, consider making use of the services of a professional financial planner, or at least an online planning service.

Deciding where to invest your money

Investment options can be a bit intimidating. There is a wide array of good choices in most countries. When you add international investments to these, your options number in the thousands. There are some easy-to-understand investment options that are low-cost and will generate good growth. However, you do need some common sense and patience.

Before choosing an investment, you should set your investment goals. These are usually time-linked in months (when saving for a holiday) or years (when saving for a house). The length of time will determine what type of investment you should make.

Short-term goals: One month to three years

If you have a goal that needs to be achieved within a period of three years, you should not be taking investment risks. That means you should not consider investments that have any exposure to shares, cryptocurrencies, property or international investment markets.

Rather, invest your cash in a money market account or an account at a bank, as these are relatively safe investments. In the case of cash investments, be especially cost-conscious, as any fees you have to pay will eat into your returns. Don't make any money market investment that incurs bank charges or fees for opening or adding to it. Most banks offer instant-access money market accounts for which they charge no fees, and which pay relatively high interest rates. Generally, you will earn higher interest rates on larger amounts and on amounts that are invested with the bank for longer periods. This means you will earn more on a six-month fixed deposit than on a 32-day notice account. Be sure to shop around and read the terms of the investment to see if there are any hidden costs or conditions that might cost you later.

You can also invest in a money market mutual fund, as these might offer you a competitive interest rate. Again, make sure that you do not pay upfront fees. It is also important to ensure that you keep your short-term money invested in the right currency. This often applies to international holiday or education expenses: if you are planning a European holiday in two years' time, it makes sense to save the money for that holiday in a euro-denominated account. In practice, you could then consider a money market mutual fund for this expense, as it is cumbersome to open a bank account in another country for a once-off purpose.

The reason why it makes sense to keep your short-term savings in the same currency as your planned expense is that you want to eliminate the possibility of a big move in exchange rates. For example, if you live in the UK and plan to study for an MBA in Europe, rather save towards this in euros so that you don't run the risk of the pound losing value just before you need to pay for your course.

Longer-term goals: Three years or more

If you are planning for a long-term goal, be prepared to take some investment risk. That means you should look at investing in shares instead of cash.

A share is the smallest unit of ownership in a company or mutual fund. You can own shares in private companies and in companies that trade on the stock market. Shares will give you three or four times more growth than cash, but investing in shares is riskier, which is why you need to invest this money for longer periods.

There are many ways to invest in shares: you can buy shares directly through an online stockbroker, via an ETF, or through mutual funds. If you are investing a relatively small amount, the cheapest and easiest investment is through ETFs. ETFs are traded on the stock market like ordinary shares, but they consist of a basket of shares in various companies. Essentially, an ETF allows you to make one investment in which you buy many underlying shares. You can invest very small monthly amounts or larger lump sums.

You can also buy individual shares directly through an online stockbroker to build your own portfolio. This means you actually own shares in particular companies of your choice. I generally recommend that if you are new to investing in shares, it is best to invest in large, well-known businesses that have been around for many years.

It always makes sense to use your own knowledge of businesses when you buy shares. For example, if you are an engineer, you might have a good insight into the building industry, so you might consider construction shares first. This requires some research on your part, as you need to be very sure of what you are buying. Individual shares can generate great returns but can also lose you loads of money if you choose badly. You should aim to buy shares in at least 15 different companies to have a properly diversified share portfolio.

If you buy shares via a stockbroker, be careful of the fees they charge per transaction and/or per year. There are some really good online trading platforms that charge very low fees to investors who want to buy shares or ETFs. When selecting an online platform, it is important to ensure that the platform is legitimate. Always make sure that the platform is regulated and registered with a recognised regulator.

You can also access shares through mutual funds. Mutual funds are also known as unit trusts or collective investment schemes (CISs), or open-ended funds. They are called open-ended investments because they have no set limit, either in time or money. These funds are generally well regulated and operated by professional investment companies. Each investor in the mutual fund is called a unit holder, and they are the only owners of the mutual fund. This is important, because it means the money in the fund will not be lost if the operator of the mutual fund goes bankrupt. The operator doesn't own the assets in a mutual fund. There are many types of mutual funds, as they represent a variety of investments, including shares, cash, bonds and property. It is important to understand that investment in a mutual fund is not the same as investment in shares; it is merely a way for many investors to pool their money to lower costs.

Because mutual funds are generally well regulated, you can rely on the information supplied in their marketing material, often called a fact sheet. The fact sheet explains the risks, costs and returns of the mutual fund. Try to invest in funds that have a track record of at least five years or more – don't simply pick the best-performing mutual fund of the moment, because the top fund today could easily be the worst fund in six months' time.

There are many thousands of mutual funds around the world. When selecting a fund that is appropriate for you, start by focusing on the time horizon for your investment. If you plan to invest for a period of five years or longer, you can choose funds that only invest in shares (also called equities). If you are looking for a fund that can invest in shares around the world, you are looking for funds that are generally called global equity funds. This means their investment options are not limited to a single country – they can select shares from around the world.

When choosing a global equity fund, I advise only considering funds that have delivered more growth than the index over five years or more.

Indices

It is worth explaining what an index is at this point because it is widely used in the world of investments. Let us consider the MSCI World Index, which represents more than 1 500 shares from more than 20 stock markets around the world. Its value is usually quoted as a number, for example 281.13. This represents the 'value' of all the shares in these stock markets and is meaningful only in that it explains whether the markets went up or down over a specific period. However, it is also a useful way to measure whether a specific investment has generated good growth over a long time.

There are not many mutual funds that have beaten the MSCI World Index over long periods, so it is advisable to do your homework. Again, be wary of costs: you should not be paying any upfront fees to invest in a mutual fund, and annual fees should be no more than 1.5% of the value of your investment per year. Over long periods (meaning 10 years or more), you should expect the MSCI World Index to grow your money by more than 6% per year measured in US dollars. This rate is not guaranteed, and you might lose money over some periods, but the longer you remain invested, the higher the chance that you will benefit from good growth. A good global equity mutual fund or MSCI World Index Fund can be a primary investment for most investors.

If you follow the investment principles set out in this chapter, you will become a very effective saver. People often try to create a sense of mystique about the investment business, but investment is not complicated at all; rather, it is difficult. And it is difficult because most people are incapable of spending less than they earn. It is difficult because they do not like to wait for five years to achieve a goal. It is difficult because they want instant gratification.

Investments require time and patience. They are your biggest allies. Short-term thinking, by contrast, is your greatest enemy.

CHAPTER 5

INVESTMENTS 101

As the world continues to deal with a major period of economic uncertainty caused by the Covid-19 pandemic, investment markets continue to be volatile. Commentators have struggled to provide sensible commentary on what's happening and what might unfold in the future. In fact, users of Dictionary.com voted for the word 'unprecedented' as the People's Choice 2020 Word of the Year. It is true that this is the first time in more than a hundred years that the entire world is facing a global health crisis simultaneously. However, stock market investors deal with a crisis almost every year and we should not be caught in the hype, as hype can lead to bad investment decisions.

During any crisis, and especially during a global pandemic, it is understandable if you feel a little at sea, and wonder if stashing your money under the mattress might not be a safer bet than investing. It is important to know that stock markets have always been volatile. The causes of the volatility tend to be varied, but volatility for investors is never unprecedented. Ultimately, stock markets are driven by people, and people have not changed at all over the past few thousand years.

We are ultimately driven by emotion in the short term and logic in the long term. As a result, people become overconfident (or greedy) when things are going well. Emotions overtake reason and people start believing that the good times will last forever. This belief becomes stronger if the good times last a long time. Those who miss out on the initial phase of a stock market boom tend to feel a sense of loss. This sense of lost opportunity, or FOMO (fear of missing out), is made far worse in the age of social media, where we observe others gloating about their successes. Unfortunately, making an investment based on FOMO is usually very risky and almost always leads to losses and regret. Typically, investment markets tend to create the greatest amount of hype just before the party ends and everything crashes. If you feel a sense of FOMO about an investment, my advice is to rather hold off on any decisions to buy into it for a few months. The party might continue for a while and you might feel silly for missing out, but the odds are almost always in your favour – and you are likely to observe a crash in prices. This might present you with the opportunity to buy into the investment at a better price. Alternatively, it might serve as a lesson in the dangers of hype in markets.

There are times when investors become too fearful, and hype causes people to stampede out of stock markets in large numbers. When a move away from the stock market gathers pace, it can cause the prices of wonderful investments to plummet below any rational basis. It is in these times that the greatest investors have been able to ignore the emotional hype and focus on a few key principles. I will outline some of these principles in this chapter. The theory behind investing is quite basic, and it is actually easy for anyone to implement over time. However, successful investing requires patience and discipline. Lack of patience and discipline is what makes it very difficult for most people to implement investment theory successfully over a long period.

The key to good investment decisions is to focus on factors that you can control. A sound understanding of how investments work is a good start. But there are other factors you can control too to ensure that your personal financial ship is able to navigate the choppy waters ahead.

From Chapter 4 you will remember that there are three basic steps to follow if you want to become financially free:

- **Step 1:** Become debt free.
- **Step 2:** Build an emergency fund.
- **Step 3:** Earn income from your assets to cover your expenses.

In this chapter we look at the third step: how to build your investment portfolio to earn an income from your assets to cover your expenses. It is important to keep in mind that the three steps need to be completed in sequence. There are many similarities between building financial freedom and building a house: if you do not build your house in the right order, it will eventually collapse. The same holds true for your financial freedom. So, only once you have completed the first two steps can you start investing your money to meet your financial objectives. The sooner you can begin this third and final step, the more time you will have to build your capital. Don't forget that time is your biggest ally on your investing journey, because you are tapping into the power of compounding to work for you. It is the superpower that every investor needs to achieve long-term success.

How to build your investment strategy

When you start building your investment portfolio, it is worth following these steps:
- **Step 1:** Define your investment objective.
- **Step 2:** Establish how much you can put away each month.
- **Step 3:** Decide what assets to buy.
- **Step 4:** Get started.
- **Step 5:** Keep going!

STEP 1: *Define your investment objective*

As with every journey in your life, you have the best chance of reaching your goal if you know where you are going. Your investment objectives will guide every decision related to your investment activities. For example, your goal might be to have a certain amount to pay for your grandchild's education in five years' time. Or you might have a long-term plan of providing for retirement. If you set a specific goal for your investment, it will help you to determine how much time you have to invest. The more time you have to invest your savings, the higher the risk you can afford. If you can afford more risk, you may get a better return on your investment!

STEP 2: *Establish how much you can put away each month*

One of the biggest money-management mistakes people make is to pay their monthly expenses (rent, medical insurance and so on) first and then spend the rest. If you want to take charge of your financial life, you need to prioritise your saving, control your spending and rethink your debt. As a general guideline, I believe investors should be saving at least 15% of their income every year.

Part of this process involves getting rid of bad debt. Do not think of investing until you have paid off your credit cards, store cards and personal loans. Interest charged on these debts is almost always higher than the earnings you achieve through saving or investing.

STEP 3: *Decide what assets to buy*

If your investment time horizon is shorter than five years, calculate how much you will have to put away monthly to reach your target. You do not have the luxury of time to make up serious investment losses, so confine yourself mainly to low-risk assets such as cash or money market funds.

A longer-term investment period – anything from five years upwards – gives you the flexibility to buy a range of assets. Generally, you can create a portfolio of assets that includes cash, government and corporate bonds, property companies, and shares. Shares and property companies tend to offer the best growth if you have a long enough investment horizon. They should do better than cash and money market investments over five years or longer. By contrast, in the short term, returns from the stock market could be quite scary. You might see a drop in share value by as much as 50% over a 12-month period. This is horrible to experience, but it is important to note that this is normal in the stock markets. You need to be prepared for the emotional roller coaster that comes with share investing. Most importantly, do not panic about your investments after they have lost a lot of money; when their value is low might be the perfect time to buy more!

If you are starting out, you may want to enlist the services of an experienced financial advisor to help you with your initial steps into the world of investments. Try to choose an advisor who will charge you an hourly consultation fee to provide you with the necessary information and recommendations. This will ensure that the advisor is as objective and unbiased as possible. It is important to remember that you remain responsible for researching every decision thoroughly. Do not rely on the advice of an advisor without understanding what they have recommended. If you want to manage your investments, you need to be informed about all aspects of your investment portfolio. I provide a summary of various investment options in Chapter 11.

STEP 4: *Get started*

Most people who start investing for the first time will be investing into a mutual fund or ETF. Fortunately, investors are increasingly being spoilt for choice when it comes to buying these investments. New fintech businesses and older financial institutions have developed very low-cost online platforms that make it cost-effective and easy for investors to buy into these with relatively small amounts of money. It is important to shop around for the best platform before embarking on your investment career. Always do some online research before using a platform. When I do research, I focus especially on customer reviews, and on articles about problems or regulatory issues. Always rely on your common sense – if something seems too good to be true, be careful!

STEP 5: *Keep going!*

To ensure that you keep up your monthly investment contributions, consider a debit order. Never scupper your long-term investment plans by cashing an investment in for a holiday or to buy a new car. And finally, be prepared for stock market crashes and try to remain invested when they happen. Sometimes it is best to keep investing aggressively during a market storm. Remind yourself in these times that your investment decision is designed to deal with many market storms over many years.

If you have investments that are not doing well, try to understand why this is so before you get rid of them – they might be poised to grow in the years to come. If you invested in a mutual fund, for example, you should compare it against its peers to get an idea of how it is really doing. If all mutual funds are doing badly, this might mean that the entire market is struggling, and this could be a time to increase your buying.

If you have extra money to invest, plan carefully how you want to allocate these extra funds and take steps to ensure that you stick to the plan. For example, if you want to invest in an ETF, then sign a monthly debit order to ensure that you implement your plan. Good plans are worthless without implementation.

Focus on the right things

Your success as an investor will probably rely on your ability to focus on the right issues rather than your ability to know everything or to be more intelligent than everyone else. There is so much information available to investors that it is easy to get lost in the noise. If you focus on the wrong issues, it is possible to completely derail your investment strategy. A great example of the importance of focus is from the Second World War. A statistician, Abraham Wald, was working for the USA on a project to study the aeroplanes that successfully returned from their bombing missions in Europe. The purpose of the study was to see if additional armour needed to be provided so that more of the planes would survive. It was not possible to simply increase the armour on the whole plane, as that would make the planes too expensive, heavy and cumbersome.

The military had already studied the surviving planes and had concluded that the armour around the areas that received the most bullet holes should be increased. But Abraham Wald recommended the opposite: he advised that the areas that had damage should be ignored and suggested that the areas with no bullet holes should be reinforced instead. His reasoning was that planes that did not return must have been hit in the areas with no bullet holes. That meant the engine, cockpit and rudder needed armour, while large sections of the wings and fuselage could tolerate significant damage without this damage affecting the plane's ability to return home.

Investors need to adopt a similar approach to investing. We need to understand that there are certain principles that are critical to our long-term success. If we focus on the right principles, we can ignore a lot of the irrelevant information that can sink our chances of success.

Basic principles of investing

There are some basic principles that everyone should understand before they begin investing, namely diversification, risk management and asset mix (or asset allocation). I focus on each of these principles in detail when summarising various investment options in Chapter 11, but I also introduce them briefly here.

Diversification

Most people believe that diversification (combining a wide variety of investments in a single portfolio) applies only within specific asset types. In other words, when you invest in shares, you should invest in a range of different shares. But diversification is a much broader concept than this. You can also diversify across asset types, across different geographies, and over time. It is important to diversify your investments as much as possible. Possibly the most important diversification is across different geographies and asset types because they all move at different times and for different reasons. When shares are falling because of a global economic crisis, bonds might be rising because governments are cutting interest rates. Over long periods, a diversified portfolio of assets will provide consistent growth at a lower risk than if you invested all your money in one country or one type of asset.

Most people do not understand the importance of diversification over time. Say you are investing in shares with a lump-sum amount. To diversify over time, the basic principle is to phase your money into the market over a few months, rather than buying all the shares in one go. To understand why this is important, consider those who invested in the US stock market in the year 2000. They invested their money in the final stages of the stock market boom that was later dubbed the dot-com bubble, when many investors believed that companies using a new business model driven by the internet were going to change the business world forever. This proved to be an accurate assessment, but most investors were eight to twelve years too early in their predictions. Many people lost fortunes when the dot-com bubble burst with spectacular losses. Those who put their money in the US market in one amount at the end of 1999 had not recovered their losses 12 years later. However, if they had invested over a 12-month period starting in

June 2000, they would have recovered their losses and made a profit in subsequent years.

In the lead-up to the year 2000, the US stock markets boomed, with shares in internet businesses doing particularly well. In March 2000, the stock markets reached their peak, with the Nasdaq technology index hitting an all-time high of 5 135.52. After the bubble burst, the index collapsed, and it only reached new highs (above 5 135.52) in 2016! However, the Nasdaq was at levels of 2 400 nine months before the crash and nine months thereafter – a difference of 50%! If you had been an investor in this index, the simple act of phasing your money into your investment over a period of months would have made a world of difference.

While the Nasdaq is an extreme example because the index consists of volatile technology companies, investors in the broader stock market had the same experience. The S&P 500 index is made up of the 500 largest companies on the US stock market. If you had invested in the S&P 500 index six months before or after March 2000, you would have bought into the index at 30% less than the peak.

The same principle applies when you invest in 'bad' times. Just as we cannot determine when the market will peak, we also cannot determine when the market will hit the bottom, so it makes sense to phase in your investments over a few months. Chances are that you will never be exactly right in the timing of your purchases, but at least you will have some capital committed before the inevitable recovery takes place. You cannot simply wait for things to get better, as this means you will be buying shares at higher prices rather than participating in – and benefiting from – the recovery.

The second form of diversification is to invest in a range of different countries. Many people around the world only invest in their home country. This is certainly true for those who live in the world's largest economies, such as the USA or Europe. While it is true that the US economy and the US stock market account for more than 50% of the world's stock market in value, this doesn't mean US-based investors should keep all their money in the USA. Many of the fastest-growing economies with the most productive populations are in Asia. Much of the world's mineral wealth is in Africa and other emerging countries. Ensuring that you have a portion of your money invested outside of your home country will potentially increase the growth of your investments while also reducing your risk. If you live in a volatile or politically unstable country, geographic diversification can be a great antidote to the uncertainty of your home base. I believe all investors should have a minimum of 25% of their investments offshore, and some might benefit from as much as 75%. We will discuss this in more detail in Chapters 7 and 9, with some examples to show how you can determine your ideal overseas allocation.

Risk management

Most investors perceive risk to be market volatility, or unpredictable ups and downs in share prices, but market volatility is only really a problem for traders or speculators because of the limited time they can invest. If you are a long-term investor, volatility presents an opportunity for you to buy great investments at a discount while others are panicking.

I believe that the impact of inflation on your assets is a far greater risk than market volatility. This doesn't mean that I advise you to ignore volatility. But I do believe that investors often focus too much on avoiding volatility rather than managing it. I view stock market volatility in the same way as I view ocean tides: you cannot control the tide, but you can build a boat that will rise and fall with the tide without sinking. In the context of investments, if your money cannot rise with the inflation rate, you are sinking. The best way to ensure that your assets can tolerate volatility is to ensure that you diversify your assets and that you are patient when markets fall.

Inflation is a different beast: it destroys the value of your money incrementally every day, so there is no major event that alerts you to the problem. It acts like a slow poison; you will only realise the impact of inflation once it is already too late, and your capital is no longer able to sustain your lifestyle. The only safe way to beat inflation is to invest in growth assets (shares and property), which are volatile by nature. People who do not understand this concept often struggle financially in retirement because they tend to avoid volatility to try to protect their wealth against inflation.

Asset mix

Your asset mix (also called asset allocation) is how much capital you have in shares, property, cash and bonds. Every person's asset allocation will be different.

In essence, most people should have a range of 35% to 75% of their investments in shares. If you have less than 35% in shares, with the balance in cash and bonds, there is little chance that your capital will outpace inflation over the long term. By contrast, having more than 75% invested in shares is classified as a high-risk strategy, especially if you require income from your capital. We will look at asset allocation in more detail in Chapters 6 and 7.

Long-term investing versus short-term trading

One of the great debates in the investment world centres on the benefits of long-term investing versus short-term trading. In the one camp you have investors like Warren Buffett as one of the champion long-termers, while George Soros is in the opposing camp. But they're both billionaires.

The track record of successful long-term investors cannot be ignored, but the argument in favour of short-term trading is far more intuitive and more easily understood. This is especially true after a market crash, when outsiders and critics wonder how long-term investors are silly enough to remain invested when stock markets are so obviously overvalued. The question they usually ask is this: 'Wouldn't it be better to sell out now and wait until a crash to reinvest at better values?'

Trading

It is human nature to want to make money as quickly and as easily as possible. And, of course, any investment method that allows you the opportunity to make returns quickly will be more attractive at first glance.

At its core, this is one of the strongest attractions of trading as an investment philosophy – it enables you to make money quickly. The philosophy of a trader is easily understood: you can make money if you are able to buy an item cheaply and sell it to someone else at a higher price.

In addition, market crashes are almost always obvious with the benefit of hindsight. Based on hindsight, we can argue that any investor with a bit of savvy should be able to anticipate a crash. This means investors could have exited the market before the crash and bought in again after the crash. Admittedly, I am substantially simplifying the case for trading, but I hope this illustrates the point that, in principle, trading is straightforward and easily understood.

Traders are able to use more complex financial instruments to profit from market crashes by 'selling short'. This means that they borrow investments from someone so that they can sell them in the hope that those investments will lose value. (This is the opposite approach to that of the long-term investor, who buys investments hoping they will gain value over time.) The short-seller will then buy the investments back at a lower price and return the investments to the owner. The difference between the price at which they sold the investments and the price at which they bought them back again would be the short-seller's profit. This is a very risky strategy, because the short-seller must pay the owner a monthly fee for the investments they borrow, so if the value of the investments goes up after the short-seller has sold them, this could cost the short-seller a fortune.

A great example of short-selling is called the GameStop short squeeze. A US-based video game retailer called GameStop caught the attention of short-sellers who believed the business was heading into difficulty. As a result, these short-sellers borrowed shares in GameStop and sold them. Once the shares had been sold, some of the short-sellers became very vocal about their concerns for the future of GameStop's business. Their aim was to use media exposure to drive the share price of GameStop down. If they had succeeded, they would have been able to buy the shares back at a much lower price than they had sold the borrowed shares initially. The difference in the sales price of the borrowed shares and the subsequent repurchase would have resulted in a nice big profit for the short-sellers. This carefully structured trading plan was destroyed by thousands of private investors who actually decided to buy GameStop shares through platforms like Robinhood. These private investors caused the share price of GameStop to rocket upwards and this caused massive financial losses for the short-sellers, who were then forced to buy the shares at much higher prices. In fact, some of them needed to pay a price that was 30 times higher than the price at which they had sold the borrowed shares.

There are many hundreds of ways to be a trader, but there is one theme that characterises most of them: they operate on a short time horizon. Traders are not making investments that will yield substantial returns after three to five years. Their time frames are typically shorter than 12 months. The fact that traders base their decisions on a short time horizon further emphasises that trading provides opportunities to make money quickly.

This ability to generate big profits in a short time was clearly illustrated by George Soros in 1992, when he made $1.1 billion in a brief period by betting that the British pound would be devalued once the British government realised it could not keep the currency artificially overvalued. Soros and his investment company essentially bet $10 billion on this view because he sold short on the pound with $10 billion. When the pound dropped, he bought back the same quantity of pounds, but he only needed to pay $8.9 billion – which meant he made a profit of $1.1 billion.

My primary concern about trading is the number of investment decisions that a trader must make in his or her career. Every investment decision is an opportunity to make a mistake. This is particularly true if you are under pressure to make money all the time. This pressure is compounded once you have made a few mistakes and the market is going against you. In this situation it is extremely difficult to remain rational and face the storm, which is why we most often read about big 'blow-ups' (losing all one's money in an investment) occurring in firms that specialise in trading.

George Soros is an excellent example of this. In the 2008/09 financial crisis, he lost a large amount of money because his predictions were wrong. These losses were instrumental in eventually causing him to retire. I know very few individuals who are successful traders with their own money, but I know many people who are successful investors with their own money.

Long-term investing

Long-term investing is less intuitive, but its essence is easily grasped. Long-term investors aim to buy an investment to hold it for an extended period until it reaches a specific target price, at which time they sell it. They usually aim to hold their investments for at least five years, a time frame that provides fewer opportunities to make investment decisions. This is a good thing, as they are less likely to be influenced by short-term events that could lead them to make irrational decisions.

Longer time frames allow investors better perspective: if you only expect to sell something in five years' time, you are less likely to react to news that might influence the share price of that investment for a three-month period. But for a trader, three months could be the equivalent of a lifetime.

I am unashamedly a fan of long-term equity investing. A good long-term investor treats each decision to buy shares in the same way as a person deciding to buy a home: you look at all the defects and positive factors of the investment, with a view to keeping it for the next 10 to 20 years.

Long-term investors only really become rich after 10 to 15 years of investing. If they invest wisely, the chances of 'blowing up' on a long-term investment are much smaller, while traders face this risk constantly. Even if the stock market doesn't perform well over lengthy periods, say 10 years, a long-term investor can still make money from dividend-paying shares over this period. Dividends make up more than 30% of the total returns earned by equity investors over the long term. This is one of the reasons I prefer long-term value investors: they focus on dividends and not merely on the 'growth story' of a company.

Of course, trading as an investment philosophy has its merits – there are thousands of people who have made a fortune through trading. At the same time there are many more traders who have lost everything and are now trying to make a living in other industries.

Cost of investments

People often ignore the costs associated with investments. Costs can mean the difference between a poor investment track record and a successful one. Many investors spend a lifetime saving diligently and investing on a regular basis, only to be severely disappointed at the pedestrian long-term growth of their investments. This is often the case when investors use financial products offered by large banks and other assurance companies. In my experience these companies are excellent marketing machines with highly paid armies of sales agents who specialise in selling expensive investment products that pay high commissions to the product providers and sales agents but deliver a lousy return for investors. I admit that I am generalising, but it is prudent to closely check all the costs of any potential investment before you take the plunge. As a guideline, avoid products on which you are charged an initial fee for starting the investment. Always be careful of a product that charges you a penalty to sell or move your investment. I believe that exit penalties on an investment are a big red warning light; I won't easily consider a product that has an exit penalty as part of its terms and conditions.

When selecting an appropriate investment home for your money, consider the following costs before making your decision:

- How much will you be charged to buy or sell your investment? There are many investment platforms that offer a wide range of mutual funds, ETFs or shares that you can buy for your portfolio. Some platforms will charge you very low fees to buy or sell these investments – it is even possible to get these transactions at no cost! While this might seem too good to be true (not a bad way to consider these offerings), some platforms have found new revenue streams that subsidise their trading costs. For example, certain shares or ETFs on the platform may attract no fees, but there might be very high fees for buying other ETFs. Alternatively, the platform may offer free trading for a limited number of investments but charge a high monthly fee to access a wider range of investments. Always do your research on consumer-education websites before deciding on a platform.
- If you invest with a platform that only offers its own products, you might get a good deal on price, but you will have to sacrifice your range of investment options. This might work for some investors who only want to buy a few different ETFs and are happy to buy them all from one company.
- Besides transaction costs, you also need to find out how much you will be charged to hold the investment every day, month or year. For example, the investment platform might charge you a fixed fee per month to keep an account. This could be $5 per month or $1 000 per

year. Other platforms might charge you a percentage of the value of your investments. If you have $100 000 invested on a platform, you might be charged 0.15% per year as a custodian fee, which works out to $150 per year. Custodian fees can eat away your growth if they are too high.

If you want to invest in ETFs or mutual funds, it is extremely important to understand their management costs. These costs differ from the trading costs a platform might charge you. In most cases, management costs are not charged as a fee that you will see on your transaction statement. The management costs are usually charged within the investment itself and are harder to track. You will generally be able to find these costs by looking for the total expense ratio (TER) of the fund or the total investment charge (TIC). This will tell you how much the fund provider is earning to invest your money, plus all the other costs that are incurred within the fund, for example trading costs, auditing fees or custodian fees. Some mutual funds will also charge a performance fee, which means the fund earns extra money if it does well. This might seem like a fair deal, but the fees on these funds often go as high as 4%, which will drag your performance down over a long period. By comparison, a low-cost ETF might only cost you 0.1% per year. This means that a high-cost mutual fund could be 40 times more expensive than an ETF!

When you choose your investments and your investment platform for your global investments, always consider taxes as part of your selection process too. Some countries, such as the USA and the UK, will charge you death duties that could be as high as 40% of some investments. In addition, you might have to sacrifice some dividend or interest income if you choose an investment in a country that charges withholding taxes on income. Other countries again might also charge you tax on your capital profits when you sell. All of these taxes will slow down the growth of your investments. That doesn't mean you should not pay some taxes, but it is worth understanding the tax implications of your investments and how you can pay the least amount of tax in a legal way.

Taking control

If you are not an investment professional, the very thought of managing your own investments may seem stressful to you. Today you might hear an expert on the radio telling you that 'equities are cheap', and the following morning you may read that 'equities are overvalued'. How on earth are you supposed to make an investment decision without completing a degree in finance?

The most important thing you can do is develop an investment strategy that suits you. This doesn't have to be complex, and it certainly doesn't require a doctorate in economics. All you need to do is apply some common sense and do a little research.

For a start, you need to understand what will drive the performance of your money over the long term. This starts with knowing the difference between good investments and poor investments. A good way to judge whether investments are good is by finding investments that have consistently managed to outperform inflation over a long period.

Shares and property companies are consistently the best investment over the long term, and cash is the worst. But as with any investment, no one can predict how share prices will move, or when; nor can anyone predict how much dividend income will be generated by your shares. In other words, there is risk associated with all forms of investment, even long-term investments. So it may not make sense to have all your capital in shares if you need income and capital preservation, but cash will not be your best growth asset. If you need income and growth, you probably need a combination of investments.

This means you need to determine the right combination of investments and decide when you should start investing. First, however, you need to be aware that market timing and the choice of individual investments will have a minimal impact on how well your money will grow over the long term. A landmark study called 'Determinants of Portfolio Performance' in 1986 by US academics Brinson, Hood and Beebower was published in the Financial Analysts Journal.[2] It found that 93.6% of portfolio movements were determined by your asset mix. This means that the primary reason a portfolio of investments moved up or down on a daily basis was determined by the

---

2 See https://www.semanticscholar.org/paper/Determinants-of-Portfolio-Performance-Brinson-Hood/ef3a2d1bfbe55685903e538bcf329993eeb958d3.

combination of asset types in the portfolio. The combination of cash, bonds, property and shares that you hold has far more impact on your portfolio growth than the selection of the right shares, property or bonds. For people who are worried about their investments, this is very powerful information. It means that you do not have to worry too much about whether the stock market is expensive or whether you should buy Amazon or Pfizer. You should rather focus on getting the right combination of assets for your investments.

Using an investment plan that focuses on an asset allocation that suits your objectives allows you to ignore much of the noise in the media. If your goal is high growth, you should allocate more money to shares. A goal of high income means more money invested in bonds and property companies with a smaller amount in shares. Once you have established your asset mix, you don't need to monitor your investments too often – you can focus on other aspects of your life. Instead of worrying about currencies, high stock markets or interest-rate changes, you can focus on your income, expenses, assets and debts, all of which you have to deal with every day, and which are under your control to some extent.

Personal values: ESG and sustainable investing

Over time, private investors have started to realise that they can use their investments to drive companies to act in a more ethical and sustainable way. The increasing effects of climate change have certainly accelerated this process. Initially, only a handful of vocal organisations and pension funds took these factors seriously, but in recent years sustainable investing or ESG (environmental, social and governance) factors have filtered into mainstream investment discussions. Sceptics initially dismissed the topic as a fad or short-term trend that would fade away. Fortunately, the sceptics have been proved wrong. Many large pension funds, asset managers, corporates and even governments are now driving sustainability as a core value in investment decisions.

The impact of this changing focus in investments is already bearing fruit in many unexpected ways: banks that previously funded large fossil fuel projects have been forced to stop supporting polluters. Manufacturers of clothes, electronics and other goods are now compelled to account for outsourced suppliers that make use of child labour or unfair labour practices. Companies that operate in corrupt countries are being pressured to account for their actions in their home countries. It is impossible for companies to ignore human rights abuses in countries where they or their suppliers operate. All these factors are driving corporates to behave better, and this could lead to potentially better investment outcomes for all investors. Behaving correctly doesn't have to be an act of charity; it can also be a profitable way of doing business. If sustainability is important to you, there are many great funds and ETFs that have a focus on ESG factors. I think it will only be a matter of time before ESG factors become a core aspect of all investments.

Forecasts and how to interpret them

We all love a good prediction, whether it is about sports results, the price of gold, or the end of the world. If you can make an accurate prediction about something significant, people will listen to you. But we know by now that predictions are generally pretty worthless; no one can accurately predict what the future will hold.

In the investment world, predictions are known as forecasting, and investors should follow any forecasts only for their entertainment value. They aren't real investment advice. Most forecasting experts have an appalling accuracy rate, and many people have lost huge sums of money as a result. Studies of the predictions of share analysts, economists and commodity analysts have shown that they are wrong more than 50% of the time. This makes their predictions effectively worthless.

Unfortunately, economics is a flawed academic discipline. Economists cannot even predict whether interest rates will rise or fall with any real accuracy. So, while it is advisable to listen to the experts, always do your own research and never base your decisions on their forecasts, as you have only a 50/50 chance of getting it right if you do, which hardly seems worth it.

CHAPTER 6

INFLATION, RISK AND ASSET MIX

Inflation is like the force of gravity. We don't think about gravity very often, but it is always there and affects most aspects of our life. Likewise, inflation has a massive impact on most aspects of our finances. If we ignore the impact of inflation, we are almost certain to destroy our standard of living once we are no longer earning an income. In most countries, your standard of living will drop by half over 10 years if your investments do not keep pace with inflation. Like gravity, inflation might not be in the news every day, but it is a dominant factor in your financial life.

What is inflation?

Inflation measures the change in prices of a range of goods and services over time. Measuring the inflation rate of a country is quite a technical exercise. If inflation is high, this means that your cost of living will increase – so you should save more, invest more and hope for better growth on your investments so that you can afford to maintain your standard of living. If inflation rates are low, this means your cost of living is likely to grow at a slow rate. But it also means you do not need to find a lot more money every year to maintain your lifestyle. However, a country's inflation rate isn't a very reliable measure of how much more you will have to spend every year on maintaining your lifestyle.

Table 6.1 shows the change in price of a cup of coffee in the USA over 50 years, to illustrate clearly how inflation can erode one's standard of living.

Consider someone who could afford to buy a cup of coffee every day in 1970. By 1980 the same cup of coffee had nearly doubled in cost. It was still the same cup of coffee, but at twice the price! And coffee is only one item: if the prices of foods, drinks, entertainment, clothes, fuel, vehicles, healthcare and medicine also double over each decade, it means your income from investments also needs to double to ensure that you can still afford the same standard of living at retirement.

Table 6.1 Inflation measured in coffee

Decade	Cost of a cup of coffee in the USA
1970	$0.25
1980	$0.45
1990	$0.75
2000	$1.00
2010	$1.25
2020	$1.79

Source: Investopedia and marketwatch.com (author's analysis)

What is the CPI?

The CPI is often quoted as a way of measuring inflation in a country. It stands for consumer price index, and it measures the change in price of a theoretical shopping basket of goods and services that most consumers need. These include food, medical care and transportation. When governments, news media and financial commentators talk about inflation, they are usually referring to the CPI.

Why is my cost of living different from inflation?

In my more than 20 years of advising people around the world about money, I have never met anyone who could measure the increase in their cost of living by the official inflation rate (usually the CPI) quoted by the government. Why is this so? Does it mean that our governments and financial institutions are deceiving us? No. Governments use the CPI to try to measure the change in price for a range of items and services across an entire country.

Rather than look at the CPI, it will be better for you to measure changes in your own cost of living every year to determine your personal inflation rate. If you monitor this annually, you will be able to make changes to your spending or investments in time to prevent permanent damage to your financial position.

What you need to know about inflation

While you certainly can't control the inflation rate, you can structure your investments so that they will generate an income to match inflation. If your investment income doesn't grow at the same rate (or better) than inflation, your ability to maintain your lifestyle will decline gradually until your whole way of life has changed for the worse. And because it happens slowly, you will not realise the severity of the problem until it is too late.

All inflation-beating investments carry some risk. It is impossible to find an inflation-beating investment that is also risk free. Many retirees start out the early part of their retired lives in a comfortable financial position. However, they often avoid investing some of their money in assets such as shares or property companies because they do not like the risk associated with these investments. So, far too many retirees invest the bulk of their money in low-risk investments such as bank accounts, fixed deposits or money market accounts. If you invest all or most of your money in this way, your capital is guaranteed to never keep pace with inflation. I believe this is a far greater investment risk than the volatile nature of the stock markets.

The volatility of the stock markets is what bothers most people. However, I see market volatility as an opportunity to buy shares in high-quality businesses at great prices and then reinvest the dividends over the next few years. When a company makes a profit, it might decide to pay some of that profit to the owners of the company (the shareholders). This payment to the shareholders is called a dividend, and the amount paid to each shareholder is determined by the amount of shares they hold. If you are a patient accumulator of shares during volatile times, you will be highly rewarded later. So market volatility is not something to be feared; rather, it is an opportunity to beef up your inflation-beating investment strategy.

Managing your risk

Many investors don't understand risk. People believe that the stock market is risky because it is constantly in motion. Human beings are not designed to deal with this constant state of movement; we naturally prefer stability and certainty. However, this constant motion is part of life for investors. It is so common that it has a name – volatility. All investors need to be comfortable with volatility, and if investors set up their investments so that these can endure some volatility, there is little danger of permanent damage when things do become volatile.

A shipbuilder who wants to build a vessel to cross the Atlantic Ocean will build a ship that can manage a few big storms during the ocean crossing. If the ship is sturdy and well built, a storm will cause some excitement on board but should not pose any real risk to the safety of the passengers. The only way passengers might be endangered is if they panicked and decided to jump overboard because they believed the ship might sink. While very few people would be crazy enough to jump off a perfectly good ship in the middle of a storm, millions of investors have been known to jump ship whenever the markets become volatile. The result is almost always the same – these investors suffer severe financial damage.

The coronavirus crash of 2020 provides a great example of this behaviour. It started in February 2020, as the world collectively began to panic about the pandemic and its potential impact on the global economy. By the end of March, the US stock market had dropped by nearly 40% within a few weeks. Millions of investors had sold their investments over a mere two weeks, and pensioners saw their retirement funds fall by $30 000 for every $100 000 they had invested.

Amid this crisis, I hosted many Zoom workshops with investors around the world, because international travel and conferences were banned. I would ask investors who had sold out when they planned to reinvest their much-reduced savings. Most told me that they planned to re-enter the markets 'when things get better'. By the end of 2020, 'things' were no better: vaccine rollouts were moving very slowly, politicians were still debating the enforced use of masks, and infections were spiking in the northern hemisphere, causing a large spike in mortality. However, the markets had rebounded very strongly. By year end, the US stock market was up by more than 15% over the year. This means that investors who had invested $100 000 on 1 January 2020 would have had more than $115 000 by 31 December 2020. Sadly, many investors who had sold out in March 2020 at a loss of 30% were still holding their money in cash, waiting for things to get better.

All investors who are trying to beat inflation will experience losses during their investment career. Any good money manager will tell you that investment risk is not a one-way street; even if you are successful, there are times when the markets will take some of your money. The real art is to ensure that these losses are manageable and that they fall within your overall investment strategy. To achieve that, begin by asking yourself five questions. Let's look at each of these in turn.

QUESTION 1: *What is the term of the investment?*
This is probably the most important question to answer. If you plan to use the money you are investing within 12 months, do not choose shares, because the risk that they will lose value in such a short period is high. If you do not know when you might need your capital, you should aim for a spread of investments. You could then access your cash investments first and give yourself time to sell the riskier investments if you need the money unexpectedly. This is especially helpful during a market downturn. The golden rule is that you can take more risk when you have more time. If you can invest the money for 10 years or longer, you can have most of your money in shares. If you need all your money in one year, you should keep all your money in cash and hunt for the best interest rate you can find.

QUESTION 2: *What is my growth objective?*
Once you have established the minimum term of your investment, you need to decide what type of growth you would like. Simply put, the higher your growth objective, the greater the risk of the investment. If you want maximum

capital growth and your term is five years or longer, you could invest in shares. If your term is three to five years, then you should look at bonds, or at a combination of shares, property companies and bonds, with the largest portion invested in bonds.

QUESTION 3: *What is the benchmark for the investment?*

A benchmark is the return objective that is set by the investment manager or product provider. In most instances the benchmark for investments will be an appropriate index or combination of indices. If you wanted to invest in a mutual fund that invests in government bonds, the appropriate benchmark is the World Government Bond Index (WGBI). Alternatively, if you invested in a diversified, balanced mutual fund, the benchmark might be 60% in the MSCI World Index (shares) and 40% in the WGBI.

It is important that you have an objective method of judging your investment performance. For example, if your investment has lost value over a year – say, a loss of 5% – you might be tempted to switch to something else that has grown over the same time. However, before making this decision, you need to establish whether your investment has, in fact, performed poorly. If you are 100% invested in shares, your benchmark is the MSCI World Index. This index tracks the largest companies in the largest stock markets in the world. If the World Index fell by 15% over the year, then your loss of 5% was actually very good. Remember, shares will always lose value in some years – that is the price investors pay for their excellent long-term growth.

According to various online dictionaries, a stock (or share) index is a series of numbers that shows the changing average value of the share prices of all the companies on a particular stock market, and it is used as a measure of how well that market is performing. So, if you read that the MSCI World Share Index is at a level of 2 895, the value of the actual number is not important. The change in value of the number is what you should focus on. To illustrate, if the value of the number was 2 000 on 1 January, and it is 2 500 by the end of the year, we know that the whole stock market has grown by 25% over the year. This means that your initial investment of $100 000 is now worth $125 000. It is worth noting that the index value is the average of all the share prices in the stock market, so the value of some shares would have increased by more than 25%, while others might have lost value over the year.

If your investment is in bonds, then the benchmark might be the WGBI, which is the bond equivalent of the MSCI World Index. As an aside, there are quite a few companies that create and monitor indices. Each company will tell us that theirs is the best index, and they will have very complicated reasons for their argument. I always look for indices that are as broad and diversified as possible. For example, I would prefer to buy the MSCI World Index rather than the S&P 500 because the S&P 500 only represents the 500 largest companies on the US stock markets, while the MSCI World Index represents more than 1 500 companies across 23 countries.

QUESTION 4: *What is the maximum loss I can tolerate?*

The maximum loss you are able to tolerate can be a difficult number to determine and is usually the focus of risk-profile tools and questionnaires. If you are the type of person who will not lose sleep if your investment has lost money over the past six months, you have some tolerance for risk. If you stay awake worrying because your index investment lost a few dollars today, and you feel that you should have kept the money in a bank account, you probably have little tolerance for risk. Unfortunately, tolerance for investment risk is hard-wired into our brains. It is very similar to someone who is petrified of moths: no matter how educated the person is about moths, if they have lepidopterophobia, they will freak out when a moth lands on them. The wiring within our brain that causes some people to panic in a stock market crash is the same as the wiring that causes others to suffer from another phobia. In other words, financial education will not stop you from panicking in a stock market crash. This is important to understand, as you are certain to panic when the markets crash if you are prone to phobias. Fortunately, most investors can tolerate some loss (like most people are not truly afraid of moths) and so can allocate a portion of their money to volatile assets.

Try to estimate the maximum potential loss of an investment before deciding where to invest your money. For example, if you want to buy shares, understand that they can lose 50% of their value in a big crash and may take a few years to recover. This doesn't mean that investing in shares is a bad idea; you simply need to be prepared for the bad times that affect stock markets from time to time.

QUESTION 5: *Do I understand the investment?*

Don't be afraid to ask what you think are 'dumb' questions about investments, because these are usually the ones that will save you. Warren Buffett freely admits that he doesn't understand tech companies, even though they are some of the greatest shares to own. So he simply doesn't invest money in them. Instead, he finds other businesses that he does understand. This strategy of avoiding investments you do not understand has worked well for Warren Buffett over the past 65 years and is worth emulating. (As an aside, Buffett's company has become a big shareholder of Apple in recent years, which might indicate that he has taken the time to understand this sector or has appointed a trusted manager to take this responsibility.)

Always remember the 'too-good-to-be-true' rule: if someone wants to sell you an investment that 'guarantees' you a return of 20% per year for the next five years, you can be certain that it's a scam. It is not wise to simply trust that a large company knows what to do with investments. That means you cannot assume that if a product is offered by a large bank that it might not be a bad investment or even a scam: many large banks have been investors in scams on behalf of their clients. If you want to know more about a prominent example of this, read up on Bernie Madoff and JPMorgan Chase.

It is difficult to make good investment decisions. However, it is not too difficult to avoid the really bad ones. Good investors aim to make the fewest mistakes possible and prefer to remain invested for as long as possible. Avoiding mistakes and remaining invested for many years is a great way to make a lot of money in stock markets. If this sounds like a sporting analogy, you are correct, because this is also the secret to winning amateur tennis matches.

Do your homework before deciding and ask all the questions you have. You will never regret knowing more about your own investments, whereas you might regret knowing too little. The Bitcoin crash of 2018 is a case in point; people invested in droves in something they did not understand, simply because its price was rising rapidly. It was a lethal event for many novice investors. People were borrowing money, cashing in their pensions and even resigning their jobs to trade Bitcoin and other cryptocurrencies. By the time the dust had settled, Bitcoin's price had fallen 80% from its peak. So if you had quit your job to cash in your retirement fund of $100 000 to become a Bitcoin investor, by the end of the crash that $100 000 would have been worth a mere $20 000 – and you would have been unemployed. I dread thinking of those who borrowed money to buy Bitcoin in the hopes that they would see a massive further price rise that would enable them to make a huge profit *and* repay their loans.

Phasing in to manage risk

A lot of research shows that a dramatic loss in the early stages of your investment's life can have a severe impact on its potential future returns. This is especially true if you are recently retired and take the decision to invest 100% of your capital immediately into your desired portfolio.

I recently met John F., a retiree who had invested all his money in a diversified portfolio in March 2008. He had a good start to his investment performance, but then the stock market crashed in late 2008 and caused a 20% loss to his portfolio. During the market crash, he still needed to draw an income to pay for his living expenses, and inflation was eroding the value of his money. This combination of events resulted in long-term losses to his capital from which he is unlikely to recover.

In contrast, Sue W. also retired in early 2008 and decided to phase the cash into her retirement investments over 12 months. She experienced no losses in the first 12 months of her retirement (despite the stock market crash), although her growth was minimal over the first year. The effect of this phasing-in strategy meant that she was buying investments during the entire market crash of late 2008 and early 2009. The fact that she invested her capital slowly into the markets during a very rocky time gave her some comfort, and she experienced a low-stress first year of retirement. Her portfolio grew by more than 10% per year for the next few years of her retirement. This impressive growth can largely be attributed to the low prices she initially paid for her investments.

Phasing in has a cost

Vanguard Group, one of the largest asset managers in the world, published a report titled 'Dollar cost averaging simply means taking risk later',[3] which looked at the long-term impact of phasing a lump-sum investment into the market over many different periods. The report showed that when an investment is immediately invested into the desired portfolio as a lump sum, there is a 66% chance that it will outperform a portfolio that is phased in over 12 months. This applies to balanced portfolios, 100% equity portfolios and 100% bond portfolios in the US, UK and Australian markets.

Most gamblers would tell you that betting your money on something that has a 66% chance of winning is considered a low-risk bet. I would agree with them. If you are an experienced investor and do not need to access your capital for at least five years, it would make sense for you to invest a lump sum at once, especially if you invest in a diversified portfolio of assets. You will get a slightly better return in most market conditions. This is especially true if you invest in a rising market.

However, none of us can predict what the market will do in future, so you cannot rely on the fact that the market has recently climbed as an indication that it will continue to do so. If you are investing during a declining market, it is very likely that phasing in will work in your favour.

What to do with a lump sum

If you are investing during extremely volatile stock market conditions, or if you are not an experienced investor, it is advisable to phase your lump sum into your preferred investment portfolio over 12 months. There is little benefit in doing this over longer periods. If you phase in your retirement fund and the market rises, you will not lose capital, but you will lose out on some growth.

Conversely, if the market crashes during the phase-in period, you will limit your initial losses dramatically. This has the benefit of being less stressful and enabling you to buy great assets at a discount to their fair price. In addition, you will be less tempted to sell your investments and remain in

---

3 Published in 2012; available online at www.vanguard.com.

cash until 'things get better'. This strategy will therefore be hugely beneficial to you over your lifetime.

Asset mix or asset allocation

Asset mix or asset allocation refers to the decisions you make about how much of your money should be invested in shares, property, cash and bonds. Your asset mix is the most important factor determining your long-term success as an investor and should be the guide for all your future investment decisions.

There are many complex financial models that can be used to determine your ideal asset allocation, but they all centre on three basic factors: how long you plan to invest (investment term), how hard your money must work (required growth) and your emotional ability to tolerate losses (risk tolerance).

In my opinion, everyone should have some investment in shares, and my view is based on some simple facts. Table 6.2 shows the growth of the main asset types that investors use to build an investment portfolio. Over many decades, global shares grow at a rate of 5.6% per year faster than inflation. This is a far better growth rate than any other asset type. By contrast, the growth of cash offers a paltry 1.2% per year. If you live in a country that charges tax on interest from cash, you might be losing money with cash investments even though you feel richer every day.

Table 6.2 Global growth of main asset types above inflation

Asset type	Long-term real growth per year
Global shares	5.6%
Global property companies	3.6%
Global bonds	1.5%
Cash (USA interest rates)	1.2%

Source: Nedgroup Investments

Unfortunately, shares are also the most volatile investments over the short term and cause investors the most consternation. They do, however, still give you the best inflation protection, and to get that inflation protection, you need a minimum of 35% invested in shares. If this is the minimum allocation, then how do you determine what to do with the rest of your capital? Start by considering those three basic factors listed above: investment term, required growth and risk tolerance.

Investment term

If you are saving for a long-term goal (more than five years) and you do not need an income from your investment, you can comfortably invest 75% to 95% of your capital in shares. The balance can be held in cash for emergencies.

If you are saving for a short period (three years or less), you should have no money in shares and all your money in cash. If you are saving for three to seven years, you could have half in shares, 25% in bonds and 25% in cash. This is also a good allocation for a long-term income-generating portfolio.

Required growth

If you are young and need maximum capital growth, you should have most of your money in shares and property companies. Conversely, if you are closer to retirement and in financial difficulty, you might require significant capital growth but cannot afford to lose any money. This means you should have a small portion allocated to shares, with the bulk in government bonds and cash. Most people need maximum capital growth, which means a long-term allocation of 75% to shares.

Putting together the perfect portfolio

Here are some tips for putting together a diversified portfolio for various financial objectives:

- Property companies or real estate investment trusts (REITs) and normal shares (equities) are an ideal combination for long-term capital growth.
- Bonds can also be included in a portfolio as a stable, inflation-beating asset.
- If you are reasonably young and looking to grow your assets without an immediate requirement for income, you could combine

an investment in shares with listed property. A sensible allocation is 75% to shares and 25% to property companies.
- If you are looking for a combination of capital growth and income, you could reduce your allocation to shares, i.e. 50% in equities, 25% in bonds and 25% in property companies. This combination should ensure that your capital grows faster than the inflation rate while generating good income.
- If you are not emotionally wired to cope with the volatility of the stock market, you could reduce your investment in shares to a minimum of 35%, increase your investment in bonds to 40% and keep your property investment at 25%.

The easiest and most cost-effective way of creating a diversified portfolio is to invest in ETFs. As mentioned in Chapter 4, an ETF is an investment that tracks an investment index (e.g. the MSCI World Index), commodity (e.g. gold) or other baskets of assets. It operates like a mutual fund but trades on the stock market like other normal shares. Look for diversified ETFs and find out how much you will be charged to have them managed before you make a decision – we will cover ETFs in more detail in Chapter 7. Your ETFs should give you the necessary equity and bond exposure, and you can then add your property exposure via a property ETF. Fortunately, there are a range of online platforms that offer very low-cost options for investors to buy and sell ETFs or shares.

When selecting an online platform, there are numerous factors to consider. Importantly, you should understand what it will cost you to buy or sell an investment. Another important detail is any ongoing cost for the platform to hold your investments in an account. This could be called a custodian fee and might be charged as a fixed fee (e.g. $50 per year) or as a percentage fee (e.g. 0.15% of the value of your investments per year). Another important consideration is where your platform is housed and who regulates it. For example, if you want to use a platform in the USA, it is important to note that it will be regulated in the USA and be subject to US tax laws. This might not be tax efficient for you, as the USA will charge death duties (also called inheritance tax, situs, federal estate tax or estate duties) of 40% on assets worth more than $60 000 for people who are not residents of the USA. So, if you live in Dubai and have a $200 000 Vanguard ETF portfolio in the USA and you pass away, your family will lose $56 000 in estate tax. The same applies to investments in the UK, but here tax is levied only on assets above GBP325 000. It is important that your investment portfolio lives in a well-regulated, tax-friendly place. I prefer Switzerland, Ireland, Luxembourg, Jersey, Isle of Man and Guernsey. They are all well-regulated and have a history of protecting investors' money. In addition, they do not levy taxes on non-resident investments. This means that investors who don't live in one of those places but have investments housed there will only be taxed in their home countries.

Gold as an investment asset

For centuries people have used gold as the ultimate hedge against unforeseen risks. In times of political upheaval, economic collapse or war, wealthy families used gold as their primary method of storing and transporting their wealth.

This changed only in the last half of the 20th century, when countries started issuing currency that was not underpinned by gold, eventually causing gold to be replaced by the US dollar as the ultimate hedge against unmanageable risks. This worked very well for more than 40 years, until the early 2000s, when a series of financial shocks around the world culminated in the global financial crisis of 2008/09.

This crisis taught the world that the worldwide financial system was not as secure as everyone had thought, and that the US dollar was also vulnerable. This realisation led to a resurgence in the value of gold, which had been in steady decline since the early 1980s. New investment instruments, such as gold ETFs, have made it a popular asset class again.

Unfortunately, gold is a complex asset class to analyse because its price is largely determined by fear. If the world is in financial difficulty and people are very worried about the future, they will buy gold at any price to protect themselves against financial ruin. However, if the economy stabilises and people regain confidence in their future financial wellbeing, the price of gold will plummet.

The US dollar price of gold has grown by 3.8% per year above inflation from 1968 to 2020. By comparison, the US stock market (measured by the S&P 500) has grown by more than 7% per year above inflation since 1928 – despite all the troubles in stock markets over that time. This is not a compelling case for gold!

Unlike companies or properties, which can generate an income while you own them, gold is a dead asset. If its price declines, you will have no income to offset the cost of holding the asset. This means that you should view gold as a form of insurance: it can form a small part of your overall portfolio, but you should not expect it to generate the bulk of your capital growth over your lifetime.

In fact, unless you are very wealthy and have more capital than you require, I would not hold gold as a permanent part of my assets. It would be better to invest in large mining houses that own a range of mines. If the price of gold starts to rise because of economic uncertainty, mining-house shares will also increase in value. If the price of gold declines again, you might hope that the management of the mining companies will still generate profits from their other mines (e.g. copper or steel).

It makes sense for very wealthy families or large retirement funds to hold a small percentage of their assets in gold. The ideal allocation to gold would range between 2% and 5% over the long term. In times of great uncertainty or financial disaster, your gold can be used as currency to buy assets that others are desperate to sell.

Those who live in politically unstable countries may choose gold to make up a larger portion of their portfolio because they cannot rely on the value of their land as a hedge against financial instability. The collapse of Zimbabwe's economy proved that land ownership is not a good store of wealth in desperate times.

I would certainly not recommend gold as a preferred asset class for trading or speculating; it is so unpredictable that you could buy gold with a view to selling it at a profit in a few months and be left holding it years later because the price collapsed soon after you bought it. This happened to those who bought gold in the early 1980s and watched its price halve over a mere few months. In such situations, you will either have to sell the gold at a massive loss or be forced to hold it for decades in the hope that its price will recover.

CHAPTER 7

INVESTING AT HOME AND OFFSHORE

Why should you invest money offshore?

It is a reality that investing always carries risks. Many people are so afraid of losing money that they prefer to keep their money in a bank account or in physical assets such as gold coins. This fear of loss is natural, but it is not a good enough reason to avoid investing. In the long term, you need to give your hard-earned savings the best chance to grow faster than inflation so that you won't need to work for your entire life. Effective investing is one of the few ways to earn money while you sleep. One of the golden rules for investing is to ensure that your money is well spread across a range of different types of investments so that you do not lose all your money if one investment goes bust. This is known as diversification and is often described as the only free lunch in investments.

Proper diversification is when you have some of your money invested in cash, bonds, property, shares and potentially some commodities (e.g. gold). It is equally important that you do not allocate all your savings to one country. People who live in a country with a small economy will be familiar with the effects of having all their investment eggs in one basket. When times are good, it can be really rewarding, but in economically difficult times it can be frightening to see the value of your assets collapse. People who live in countries with larger economies that are more stable might feel more protected against volatility, but even then, they are probably experiencing a false sense of security. Consider what happened to the stock market of the world's largest economy for the decade starting in the year 2000: investors who owned the 500 biggest shares in the USA (S&P 500 index) lost 1% per year of their money over a 10-year period. Considering that inflation destroyed another 2.4% per year of the value of their money, these investors lost 3.4% per year in 10 years. However, US-based investors who had some money invested outside of the USA would have fared much better. The world's stock markets (which include the USA) collectively delivered a positive return of 1.1% per year over the same decade. If these investors had added some emerging market investments, their returns would have been rewarding indeed. Emerging markets delivered 10% per year in the decade when the USA lost 1% per year. A properly diversified global portfolio that included cash, global bonds and shares across the world would have delivered more than 5% per year.

Home bias

It is true that we all prefer to invest in what we know best. That means we would feel most comfortable if all our money were invested in our home country. In most countries, people have too much money invested in their home stock markets. It is a reality that most of us would only seriously consider investing outside of our home country if we were worried about the future of our country.

Table 7.1 shows how much various countries contribute to the value of the world's stock markets and then compares this with how much pension funds in those countries allocate to their local stock market. In the USA, for example, pension funds allocate 62% of their money to the US stock market even though the USA only accounts for 53% of the world's stock market value. Given the size of the US market in comparison to the value of the worldwide market, this home bias is not too bad. But consider Australia, which only accounts for 2% of the world's stock market value: Australian pension funds allocate more than 50% of their money to Australian shares. This is a clear indication of home bias and could pose real risks to Australian investors in the event of an economic collapse in that country. Given Australia's reliance on mining, any deterioration in the mining sector will be bad for Australian investors.

Table 7.1 Home bias in action

	USA	UK	Japan	Canada	Australia	South Africa
Share of the world stock market	53%	6%	8%	3%	2%	0.5%
Proportion of pension fund investments allocated to home stock market	62%	36%	34%	21%	52%	65%

Source: FTSE Russell and Willis Towers Watson (author's analysis)

I am not suggesting that you should only consider the value of your home stock market in proportion to the value of the world stock markets when deciding how much to invest in your home country. There are some very good reasons for keeping extra capital at home, and this is especially relevant if you plan to spend the remainder of your life there. Where you plan to spend your time (and money) will have a big impact on where you should invest. For example, an Australian who is 70 years old and plans to live out her life in Australia should not have 98% of her investments in global markets – as suggested by the information in Table 7.1. She can have a significant portion of her capital in Australia because she will spend her money in that country. However, if she has children or grandchildren who live overseas and she wants to leave them an inheritance, it makes sense to have a portion of her money overseas to protect against the potential collapse of the Australian currency or a long-term economic recession. I think Table 7.1 is a useful guide that may help you realise that you should have some money overseas, and if your country's stock market is small (as is the case in Australia), you should have more money overseas than a US-based investor, whose home market is large by comparison.

There are more factors to consider when allocating investments overseas, and I believe every investor should have a clear method for determining the ideal international proportion of their assets. If you do not have a clear methodology, you are more likely to be influenced by short-term events that will cause you to make emotional decisions rather than rational long-term decisions that work best in the world of money.

Ideal allocation to overseas markets

In Table 7.2 I show a suggested allocation to local and international markets based on your financial position. As we are all in different stages of life and have differing financial objectives, these guidelines might not be an ideal fit for you right now, but they can be a valuable starting point for considering overseas investments.

Table 7.2 Suggested allocations to local and international markets

Financial position	Amount allocated to home market	Amount allocated to overseas investments
Retiring with just enough money	75%	25%
Planning to leave some money to children	50%	50%
Planning to leave money to potential grandchildren	25%	75%

If a 65-year-old man wishes to retire with just enough money, Table 7.2 indicates that he should keep the bulk of his money in his home country. He will consume most or all of his money during his lifetime. This means the time frame of his capital is limited to the remainder of his life in retirement (around 30 years). Importantly, the bulk of his capital will need to generate an income, and this means he must balance the need for growth with the need to limit losses. These are always opposing goals: If you aim for higher growth, you will have more risk. If you need income from your capital, you cannot afford too much risk because you will need to draw on your money to fund your monthly expenses. So the diversification benefit of investing a portion of money overseas is helpful to reduce the effects of a potential collapse in your home country. However, investing overseas introduces a different risk, called currency risk. If this retiree were to invest all his money overseas and decide to draw on his savings every few months to fund his expenses, he would be exposed to the fluctuations of his home currency against international currencies. He could have a real problem if his home currency appreciates in value against international currencies at a time when he needs money, and he might lose 10% to 20% of his income simply because of currency movements. It is normal for currencies to fluctuate, and this can cause a lot of uncertainty for retired investors. To avoid this risk, it is worth retaining a significant portion of assets in your home country to ensure certainty regarding your monthly income.

If you are planning to spend a portion of your time outside of your home country every year, you will need to allocate enough money overseas to cover your expenses when you are away from home. Some people like to follow the sun and spend their time between the northern hemisphere and the southern hemisphere to avoid winter. These 'swallows' will need to invest a larger portion of their money internationally than other retirees who remain in their home country permanently. A retiree who splits her time equally between Cape Town, South Africa, and Sotogrande, Spain, will need to ensure that she has sufficient capital invested in rands to cover her South African expenses for half of every year, and sufficient euros to cover her expenses in Spain for the remainder of the year. If she plans to spend the last years of her life in this way, she could consider investing 50% of her assets in a pure global portfolio, with another 25% in South Africa and the remaining 25% in Europe.

Some parents plan to send their children overseas for their tertiary education. International student fees are typically double those charged to local citizens. This means that parents need to increase their international investment allocation substantially so that they can fund their children's education. These education expenses will need to be paid at very specific times and therefore parents should also aim to avoid the impact of currency fluctuations, as these could cause university costs to increase substantially simply because of a depreciation in the value of their home currency at the wrong moment. If you plan for your child to attend a European tertiary institution, it makes sense to have an investment in euros to fund this education cost at no currency risk.

Another factor to consider is the impact of interest rates. At the time of writing, interest rates in the USA, Europe and Japan were extremely low or even negative! If your home country offers relatively high interest rates on cash, it might make sense to increase your allocation to cash at home and to avoid investing in overseas cash until interest rates rise to normal levels. One efficient way to do this is to skew your allocation to international shares. To balance out your entire portfolio, you can reduce your allocation to domestic shares in favour of local cash, bonds and property.

Another factor to consider in your overseas investment allocation is the comparative safety of your home country. Is your home country politically stable? Are laws consistently applied and enforced? What about the management of the economy: Is it favourable to investors? Compare the relative stability of countries such as Switzerland and Singapore with places such as Hong Kong and Zimbabwe: property rights, law enforcement and political stability are far greater in Switzerland and Singapore. If your home country is stable, there is an argument for retaining more capital at home as a safety measure. If you live in an unstable country, it is worth reducing your local investments in favour of more international assets to reduce your overall risks. It would also be worth reconsidering your asset allocation: you might wish to reduce your exposure to illiquid assets such as private (unlisted) businesses and physical properties, because these might be difficult to sell in periods of economic or political instability.

> GENERAL EXAMPLE OF AN INTERNATIONAL ALLOCATION
> If I were to offer a general guideline to an investor who wanted to balance the need for income at retirement with the need for growth and the need for proper global diversification, I would aim for 50% of my assets to be invested at home and 50% overseas. American investors might choose a greater allocation to the USA, although I am not sure this is wise: the political landscape in the USA is changing, and this could pose some long-term risks to investors.

Where you live and where your money lives

One important and often overlooked consideration is that your money can live in a different place from where you live. There are some good reasons to move a portion of your capital to a different country from where you live, but there are also some potential pitfalls to avoid when making decisions about this. If you are building your wealth and want to ensure that you get the best combination of capital growth at the lowest possible risk, you need to plan for events that are impossible to anticipate. In recent times, we have all been provided with a frightening example of this type of event through the Covid-19 pandemic. We have seen how some countries and their economies were severely affected while others survived relatively intact. Besides such events, other factors such as the financial stability of a country or political uncertainty are critical risks for investors to consider. These risks are a reality worldwide, so investors need to plan for the worst and hope for the best. This means ensuring that a portion of your assets live in a different country from you. To be clear, I am not suggesting that you invest in dodgy tax havens for the sole purpose of evading taxes in your home country. This type of thinking is short-sighted because legitimate taxes contribute to a stable and growing economy, and this is critical to the health of your local investments. However, if you live in places that have an unstable political climate, such as Zimbabwe or Hong Kong, the risks of irrational or illegal actions by politicians are so high that you need to move your money to a safer haven.

When I speak to people about global investing for the first time, I often emphasise that although countries such as the USA, the UK and mainland Europe might seem like sensible and safe places for one's money, they pose significant tax risks to non-resident investors. One of the biggest drawbacks is that they charge non-residents an inheritance tax on any money invested in that country. These inheritance taxes can be very steep (ranging from 30% to 60%) and are levied even on relatively low-value assets. For example, if you own a Vanguard S&P 500 ETF in the USA and are living in South Africa or Australia, you are liable for inheritance tax of 40% on all amounts over $60 000. The rate is even higher in some European countries. It is important to consider countries that do not charge inheritance taxes to non-residents. There are some important points to note when making this decision, as some places will treat investors more fairly than others. Non-resident investors lost millions when Cyprus was in a financial crisis in 2012/13. Wealthy investors who had money deposited in Cypriot banks lost a significant portion of their money, as it was used to bail out the banks themselves. Other countries have developed a reputation for offering privacy to money launderers and other criminals. The OECD Global Forum consists of over 160 countries that are working on eradicating offshore tax evasion. As part of this initiative, some tax havens are blacklisted as uncooperative or non-compliant. When this happens, it becomes very difficult for financial institutions in other countries to deal with money from blacklisted jurisdictions. Law-abiding private investors may find themselves in an administrative purgatory if their money is housed in one of these blacklisted countries and they are unable to get the money transferred to their home country or to any other reputable destination. For this reason, it is important to ensure that the chosen home for your overseas investments is not on any OECD blacklists.

Besides inheritance taxes, you also need to consider the legal processes involved in the event of your death. If you have money invested overseas, you need to know what will happen to those investments if you pass away. Do you require a will in that country, or is a will from your home country acceptable? In addition, is a local lawyer or probate specialist required to help you? What documentation will your beneficiaries need to provide to your offshore investment company in the event of your death?

I prefer investments in countries that have a long history of good investor protection in the form of financial regulations that are implemented rigorously by competent regulators and legislators. In addition, I prefer investments in countries that are politically stable and economically prosperous. This ensures that politicians take the necessary steps to protect their financial industry and will not revert to populist policies that could be detrimental to non-resident investors. My preferred countries (at the time of writing) are Switzerland, Ireland, Luxembourg, Isle of Man, Jersey, Guernsey and Malta. Remember too that you will eventually pay taxes on your investments. Ideally, of course, you want to pay taxes in one country only.

Trusts, foundations, companies and mutual funds

In some instances, you might consider using legal structures to house your assets. This could be as simple as owning a mutual fund or an ETF instead of owning shares. This is beneficial because a mutual fund that is domiciled in a country such as Ireland or Luxembourg will protect you from the taxes levied in countries such as the USA or the UK. For instance, if you find an Ireland-domiciled mutual fund that invests in large US-based companies, you do not have to be concerned that your estate will be taxed at 40% of your investment value when you pass away. It is important to note that you are still the owner of the mutual fund and so you might need to pay inheritance taxes in your home country, but this is much better than paying taxes twice! Besides saving on inheritance taxes, you will also avoid paying taxes when a mutual fund decides to buy or sell shares within the fund. Many countries charge capital gains tax (CGT) on profits from the sale of an investment, and the mutual fund will shield you from these interim taxes. You might still be liable for CGT, but this will only become payable once you decide to sell the mutual fund and have made a profit from the transaction. This means you can anticipate and plan for these taxes.

In some instances, parents or grandparents have money they would like to leave to future generations. This can be a tricky and complicated exercise, because the money needs to move from one generation to the next in the most efficient and tax-effective way possible. Some people might also worry about transferring their assets to family members who are too young, or are mentally incapacitated, or have problems with substance abuse. If you are in a position where you have a relatively substantial sum of money ($1 million or more) that you would like to leave to future generations in your family, you can consider starting a trust or a foundation.

Trusts

A trust is a centuries-old legal structure. Its primary purpose is to ensure that the assets of one person can be managed and preserved for the benefit of and use by current and future family members and others. Typically, a person who starts a trust (called the settlor) will form the trust with the assistance of legal specialists and potentially some independent financial or legal experts. These people are called trustees. At the time the trust is formed, the settlor will write down how he or she wants the money to be managed and, importantly, who can benefit from this money. The written instructions are captured in a trust deed, and these instructions can include specific conditions on how and when the money may be used. Trusts are very flexible and can accommodate a wide range of instructions from a settlor, but they must be legal instructions. In addition, trusts can be the owners of companies, physical property, shares, bank accounts and almost any other asset. The main advantage of a trust is that the settlor moves the money out of his or her name into a legal vehicle that can live for a very long time. This means the settlor can be sure that the money will be correctly used for the benefit of future generations (called beneficiaries). In some instances, there are significant tax advantages from a trust, because inheritance taxes will no longer be a concern as trusts can live for generations. The two main problems with trusts are the costs of the trust and the fact that the settlor no longer has control of the assets in the trust.

Some trusts can be expensive to set up and maintain. It is usual for a trust to cost between $3 000 and $5 000 to set up, and the same amount per year to administer. If trusts own a variety of assets (including properties and businesses), the running costs can be much higher. For this reason it makes sense to use a trust only when you plan to invest a large sum of money, so that the costs do not erode the value of the capital over time. I believe an amount of $1 million is the ideal minimum for a trust. However, you could start with a smaller amount if you believe the asset in the trust will grow substantially in a short time – for example, if you own shares in a company that is growing rapidly.

It is important to know that when the settlor of the trust transfers money or other assets into the trust, the ownership of the assets moves from the settlor to the trust. From the time the trust owns the assets, it is up to the trustees to decide how the money is managed. The trustees need to be guided by the written wishes of the settlor (these are usually recorded in a trust deed), but they also have a duty to act in the best interests of the beneficiaries and comply with all applicable laws. This can sometimes cause conflict between trustees, beneficiaries and the settlor of the trust. Therefore, it is important for the settlor to create a very strong and detailed trust deed to ensure that all his or her wishes are carried out in the years ahead.

If you are planning to use a trust for your overseas investments, it is important to remember that the trust might live beyond your grandchildren's lifetimes. This means you should be clear on the main principles and purposes of the trust but be careful of being too restrictive. Consider the wealth impact on Zimbabwean families who had family farms owned by trusts: many trust settlors stipulated that the trust may never sell the family farm, and this stipulation caused financial devastation when Robert Mugabe allowed his political cronies to steal the farms. I believe it is always better to stipulate a principle rather than a rule. For example, you could stipulate that the trustees may only pay out half the income from the trust every year to beneficiaries. In the example of the Zimbabwean farming families, the settlor could stipulate that the farms should not be sold unless there are potential legal, political or economic changes that would destroy their value.

As a trust might remain in existence for many generations, the choice of home or domicile for the trust is critical: you need to choose a country that is stable and has a strong legal framework for regulating trusts. This is great protection against rogue trustees or rogue politicians. I prefer Switzerland, Jersey, Guernsey and the Isle of Man for overseas trusts. As a final note, it is important to get proper legal advice before you start a trust. Some countries do not legally recognise trusts or, alternatively, they tax beneficiaries excessively on any capital or income received from trusts.

Foundations

Some countries offer an alternative to trusts. These entities are called foundations. Foundations have some similarities with trusts because they are also started by a founder or settlor and can also have beneficiaries. However, a foundation is also like a company because it is incorporated even though it has no shareholders. There are many similarities between trusts and foundations, and their drawbacks are also similar. In some countries, foundations are primarily used as non-profit or charitable vehicles for wealthy families to fund worthy causes.

An alternative structure to a trust or foundation is a company that is domiciled in an offshore jurisdiction. If your company is domiciled in Jersey, for example, it can start to buy shares, mutual funds or ETFs without any concern for interim CGT or inheritance tax issues. The reason this works is because a company is a separate legal entity from you and therefore it will not pass away when you do. Moreover, if the company 'lives' in an offshore centre, it will not be subject to inheritance taxes or CGT in countries like the USA or the UK. This provides some real benefits to investors who want to house their assets overseas without worrying about inheritance taxes in the USA or the UK. However, it is important to remember that the company is owned by you, and when you pass away this asset could be subject to inheritance tax in your home country. Similarly, if you sold the company or closed it down, you might be subject to taxes.

Families with relatively large asset values ($5 million or more) might find it sensible to start a family trust that owns one or more companies. This creates the possibility for the trust to start a property company, a private equity company, and an investment company that owns ETFs and mutual funds. The benefit of this type of structure is that it separates the different asset types and their management from the administration of the trust. Often the settlor or beneficiaries might be directors of the underlying companies so that they can manage these assets without incurring additional administration costs from the trustees of the main trust. It is worth repeating that this type of structuring can be expensive and complicated, so proper legal advice is critical.

What currency is appropriate for your overseas investments?

When discussing overseas investments with people, I find that one of the main questions will centre on the choice of currency for their investments. We often debate issues such as the future of the dollar or pound, the potential collapse of the euro, and the risks of emerging market currencies. I believe it is impossible to accurately predict the direction of most currencies over any length of time. Trying to determine if the dollar will fall because of all the extra money supply being injected into the US economy is extremely difficult. If you were to avoid the dollar, what currency would you choose? If you select the euro because you are worried about the dollar, how would the euro be affected by a dollar collapse? What about the potential fragmentation of the eurozone?

It is worth noting that some currencies will devalue over time when their inflation rate is higher than their trading partners' inflation rates. For example, if inflation in South Africa is at 4% and inflation in the USA is at 2%, it is reasonable to expect that the rand should devalue against the dollar by at least 2% per year over the long term. However, over shorter periods, many factors could cause the rand to rise, or to fall much further against the dollar.

Trying to predict the direction of the largest currencies in comparison to each other is impossible. Many studies have shown that professional economists have been terrible in their currency forecasts over many years. In most instances, you would achieve more accuracy with a prediction than an economist if you were to flip a coin! Rather than rely on economic predictions to determine the currency of your overseas investments, I suggest you focus on your own requirements instead. For instance, if you plan to spend a portion of your lifetime away from your home country in Europe, it might be worth having a euro-denominated offshore portfolio. Similarly, if you are planning for your children to study in the UK, then you should have a GBP-denominated portfolio. If you have no plans to spend time or money in a specific country (other than your home country) and you are simply looking to build a properly diversified asset base, I suggest a dollar-denominated portfolio. This doesn't mean that your entire overseas asset base will be in the USA; you should still select a globally diversified portfolio of investments, but the price of all these investments can be denominated in dollars. For example, if I choose an ETF that is invested in the MSCI World Index, I will be buying something that represents hundreds of shares in more than 20 countries. However, I can choose to buy the ETF in dollars or GBP or euros. In this instance, I would buy the dollar version, because the US has the largest stock market in the world and therefore more than 50% of the shares in the World Index will be priced in dollars. This means that more than 50% of the portfolio will not be affected by exchange rate movements. If the dollar collapses, it means that the portion of the MSCI World Index that is denominated in other currencies will become more valuable when converted to dollars. If the dollar becomes much stronger against other currencies, it means that the non-dollar portion will lose value. In such scenarios it helps that more than 50% of the shares are already in the USA.

If you want to invest a relatively large amount of money overseas and can buy multiple investments in different currencies, then it makes sense to ensure that you have exposure to investments that are denominated in dollars, GBP and euros. Whatever your choice of currency for your overseas investments, try to select a currency that is relatively stable. This means you should choose a currency from one of the biggest economies where the environment for legal and political standards is stable. I am uncomfortable about selecting a country whose political leaders can change laws or economic policies without being challenged in court. That is why I would avoid Hong Kong, Dubai and any dictatorship as a home for my money. If a country's leaders can change rules about investments overnight, this could be very costly.

Different markets with different opportunities

There are many different stock markets around the world. Investors who want to buy shares in these different markets are often surprised at how complex this process can be. A stockbroker who wants to offer clients access to shares in many different countries needs to set up relationships within the stock markets of those countries individually. In some instances, this can be relatively quick and cost-effective but not always. That means larger stockbrokers tend to have access to a wider range of countries. In some instances, a company that is listed in a small economy might decide to list itself on more than one stock exchange simultaneously. This is called a dual listing and is quite common for large companies that were started in countries such as China, South Africa and Australia. The dual listing allows investors to buy the shares of these dual-listed companies on larger stock exchanges in the UK or the USA, and it makes it easier for more global investors to access larger, high-quality companies from smaller economies. I make this point because you might want to buy some investments in developing countries, and it is worth remembering that you could access them via stock exchanges in countries such as the USA, the UK and Canada.

We often read about developed markets and emerging markets or the Dow Jones and the Nasdaq indices. It is worth understanding what these markets are and how they differ before building your own investment portfolio so that you achieve the best returns at the lowest possible risk.

Developed markets

A developed economy is typically characterised by a relatively high level of economic growth and a secure political environment where capital and people can be moved with relative freedom. Developed economies have some common characteristics: they are usually politically and economically stable, and their legal system is well structured, with good balance between legal protection for citizens, the state and business. They often offer their citizens good social support, which includes access to good healthcare, education and varying degrees of social welfare where needed. Some developed economies are quite small, while some emerging economies such as China and India are enormous and growing rapidly.

If you want to invest in developed markets only, you can buy ETFs that track the MSCI World Index. This index consists of more than 1500 companies that are listed on more than 20 stock exchanges in developed markets such as the USA, the UK, Japan, France and Canada. If you invest in this index, you are primarily buying into larger companies; the average value of the companies in this index is around $33 billion.

Emerging markets

According to various online dictionaries, an emerging market economy is described as the economy of a developing nation as it engages more with global markets as it grows. Emerging market economies share some but not all of the characteristics of developed market economies. Very often emerging markets are fast-growing economies with a large and growing population. They are generally riskier and more volatile than a developed economy, but they also can offer more opportunities for capital growth. Historically, emerging market economies were smaller than developed economies, but this has changed over time. Many investors still classify China as an emerging market even though it is in a race with the USA to be the largest economy in the world. I prefer not to be too academic about these things, as I believe developed economies are generally well established with stable political and legal structures. In addition, a greater portion of their population have access to basic services and education. Emerging markets might represent the future titans of the world, but they pose more risks to investors, especially in countries where the rights of citizens and businesses are limited in favour of the rights of the state. If you want to invest in emerging markets, you can buy an ETF that invests in the MSCI Emerging Markets Index. This index consists of more than 1 300 companies listed on more than 25 stock markets in emerging market countries such as China, Taiwan, South Korea, Brazil and India. The average value of the companies in this index is more than $5 billion. These companies are quite a bit smaller than the average size of companies in the MSCI World Index. Since the year 2000, emerging markets have generated more than 9% growth per year, which is more than 3% higher than the world markets, but it is worth noting that the volatility of emerging markets is higher than that of the developed markets. In a huge stock market crash like the global financial crisis of 2008/09, you would have lost more than 65% in the emerging markets while the developed markets lost around 57%.

World markets

It is possible to buy an ETF that combines emerging market and developed market investments. Somewhat confusingly, the developed market index is called the MSCI World Index, while the index that represents developed markets plus emerging markets is called the MSCI All Country World Index (ACWI). This index consists of more than 3 000 companies listed on 50 stock exchanges around the world.

The Dow Jones, S&P 500 and Nasdaq indices

The US market makes up more than 55% of the world stock market value. This means that global investors tend to monitor this market more closely than any other because the direction of most stock markets will be determined by the direction of the US market in the short term. For instance, if the USA experiences a big stock market drop, it is almost guaranteed to cause all the major stock markets in the world to drop simultaneously. Many investors will be familiar with the Dow Jones, Nasdaq or S&P 500, as these are the primary stock market indices in the USA. The S&P 500 is probably the most relevant of all the US indices, as it tracks the 500 largest companies listed on the US stock exchanges. The Dow Jones Industrial Average is usually referred to as the Dow Jones and consists of 30 large listed US shares. It was started in the late 1800s and is still widely quoted in the media, even though it is not a very scientific measure of the direction of shares in the USA. I would generally avoid ETFs that track this index in favour of the S&P 500. The other popular index in the USA is the Nasdaq Composite (usually simply called the Nasdaq), which tracks most of the companies listed on the Nasdaq stock exchange. Many of the biggest tech companies are listed on the Nasdaq, and so it is often described as the tech index because tech companies represent such a large portion of the value of this index. Investors who want to monitor the tech sector often focus exclusively on the Nasdaq rather than the S&P 500 or Dow Jones. It is worth noting that most of the big tech companies are also represented in the S&P 500, which is why I prefer it over the Nasdaq, as I favour diversification within my investment portfolio and do not want to allocate too much money to one sector or one country. For investors who only want to buy one globally diversified investment, I would consider an ETF that tracks the MSCI ACWI.

CHAPTER 8

BUILD YOUR GLOBAL PORTFOLIO

The key to managing a private investment portfolio is to build a diversified investment portfolio while limiting your transaction costs and the time you need to spend researching and monitoring your specific investments. If you were to build a portfolio of individual shares for a global investment, I anticipate that you would need to own shares in at least 50 companies listed on various stock exchanges around the world to achieve proper diversification. It would cost you a fair amount in transaction charges to buy each share, and you would need to spend a lot of time researching the companies before making your purchases. Also, your research responsibility would continue on an annual basis as you would have to monitor each of the 50 companies to be sure that they are still worth holding for the long-term. If you are a private investor managing your own global investments, I would suggest limiting your purchases of direct shares for your global portfolio.

It can be much more cost-effective to buy ETFs, mutual funds or investment companies instead. I believe you can buy a total of six individual investments (ETFs and investment companies) in one portfolio that would give you global diversification and the potential for good capital growth. This strategy will limit your transaction costs (because you only need to buy six investments) and your research time.

If you want to construct your own portfolio, it is worth remembering a few key factors:
- Where your portfolio lives (the jurisdiction) is very important.

- The platform you use to house your portfolio should be cost-effective, reliable and well regulated. In addition, it should be easy to use and provide good service if you have a problem.
- Your portfolio must be well diversified. This includes the types of assets and geographies into which you decide to buy.
- Be careful of big market trends that might affect your portfolio performance in the short term. For example, if interest rates are very low globally, central banks may raise interest rates while you are trying to invest. Rising interest rates can cause share prices to fall. In this instance it is wise to rather phase in your purchases over 12 months.
- Consider investing at least half of your money in indexed investments. For example, you might buy a mutual fund or ETF that tracks the MSCI ACWI to get exposure to an investment that tracks global shares. This one ETF will give you an exposure to more than 3 000 shares across the world and will be managed at a much lower cost than most mutual funds or other financial products. This type of investing is called passive (or index) investing.
- If you choose to invest 50% of your money in indexed investments, you can invest the balance in actively managed investments. I discuss these in the section that follows.

Indexed investments and active investments

Historically, most mutual funds, share portfolios and other investment products offered by stockbrokers, banks, insurance companies or large asset managers have been active investments. These products were sold on the basis that professional fund managers are able to select the right individual investments and combine them in one package that will outperform an index over the long term. Unfortunately, this has proven to be a difficult promise to keep. When stock markets were far less efficient and less well-regulated than today, it was easier for fund managers to beat the index. Cynically, one could argue that their job was easier because they could trade on information that was not freely available to other investors. With the advent of the internet and better regulation around inside information, it is now much easier for anyone to access the same information about companies at the same time. With a more level playing field, fund managers are finding it very difficult to justify their high fees for below-average performance.

Index investments generally attract far lower costs than active investments. They are usually offered as ETFs or mutual funds. They are designed to track a specific basket of investments such as the largest 500 shares in the USA (called the S&P 500 index) or the biggest companies in emerging markets (called the MSCI Emerging Market Index). Brilliant investors like Warren Buffett have often promoted the virtues of index investing for private investors as it is very difficult to grow money faster than the index. Over the last few decades, index investments have begun attracting large amounts of money from all types of investors as the benefits of index investing have become more widely known. A great way to measure how difficult it is to beat the index is to look at the SPIVA report, updated regularly by S&P Dow Jones Indices. This report shows that very few active managers can beat the index over longer periods: in most markets around the world, fewer than three fund managers out of ten do. This is a real indictment of the entire stockbroking and fund management industry, and a very good argument for only investing your money in an index portfolio. This type of investment is becoming increasingly viable now that investors can buy balanced ETFs that own a share index combined with a bond index in one low-cost ETF. It means that instead of investing in different ETFs to create your own balanced portfolio, you can have an entire diversified overseas portfolio with one simple ETF. Your transaction costs will be low, and the effort required to monitor the investment will be minimal. Most importantly, if you review the SPIVA report, there is a very good chance that you will beat most global balanced fund managers over the next 10 years.

Investment trusts or investment companies

There are specialised investment companies (also known as investment trusts) that are listed on the stock exchange and are traded in the same way as normal shares. Their purpose is to manage portfolios of investments for shareholders. The oldest investment company was started in 1868 and is listed on the London and New Zealand stock exchanges.

These companies are primarily designed for private investors who want access to a range of high-quality investments that might not be accessible to them as direct investors. Investment companies are listed on a stock exchange and are well-regulated, relatively transparent investment vehicles for private investors. They are extremely flexible and can access a wide range of investments, including private companies. In addition, they can borrow money against the value of their assets. There are many different types of investment companies; some are very specialised and will invest only in certain sectors of the stock market or in certain geographic areas, while others are more diversified and flexible in their investment approach.

One primary difference between an investment company and a mutual fund is that the assets within the investment company are fixed. This means that when investors want to exit the investment company, they simply sell their shares on the stock exchange (like any normal share) and receive their money from the buyer. This transaction will have no effect on the value of the assets within the investment company. By contrast, in the case of investors exiting a mutual fund, they sell their units and the mutual fund will pay them from the assets of the fund. This means that large outflows or inflows can affect the asset value of a mutual fund. If many people sold out of an investment company at the same time, the share price might drop substantially, but the value of the assets would be unaffected. This is called a closed-ended fund. I have an affinity for this type of investment for private investors because I like the fact that the managers of these companies can maintain a long-term focus on their investments without needing to manage outflows during a market crash. As with any type of investment, there are good funds and bad ones, so you need to do your homework carefully. I generally prefer the low-cost global funds, and two of my favourites are Scottish Mortgage (listed in 1909) and Personal Assets Trust (listed in 1983). Scottish Mortgage, for instance, has a very long history of beating the global stock market index and has a running cost of 0.36% per year. The fees are comparable to many index-tracking ETFs and the long-term performance is compelling. But its performance could collapse three days after you read this book – so do your own research, be careful and be sure to spread your investments. And never put all your eggs in one basket!

Why consider active investments?

The fees for many actively managed funds are reducing constantly. The pressure of competing with low-cost index-tracking funds has helped to drive costs down. This is hugely beneficial to all investors. I believe that fees are one of the reasons why fund managers struggle to beat the index. If their fees are reducing, it means they have a chance of delivering better returns. In addition, I believe a good fund manager can deliver decent growth at potentially lower risk than the index. For example, Personal Assets Trust delivered growth of more than 7% in 2020, while the index lost more than 9%. Similarly in 2018, the index lost more than 9% while Personal Assets Trust only lost 3%. However, in rising markets, Personal Assets Trust tends to underperform the index, often substantially. That means I would consider a good fund manager to be valuable if I could get most of the returns of a rising market, while losing less than the market when prices fall.

In addition to risk management, good fund managers can access larger private companies that are not listed on the stock exchange. There is a growing trend for great businesses to avoid listing on the stock exchange because the costs and hassles of being listed are enormous. Also, many good private companies can access capital cheaply from other investors and banks without needing to list on a stock exchange.

Finally, I like paying fund managers to access investments in inefficient or smaller stock markets where quality information on companies might be limited. This is particularly valuable in emerging markets, where specialist fund managers can generate better returns than the index.

> ### MY PERSONAL GLOBAL PORTFOLIO
> Given my preferences for index investing and diversification, and my limited faith in the value of most fund managers, here is the global portfolio that I have constructed for my own investments:
> - 40% of my global portfolio is in an ETF tracking the MSCI World Index;
> - 20% is in an ETF tracking the MSCI Emerging Market Index;
> - 20% is in Scottish Mortgage Investment Trust; and
> - 20% is in Personal Assets Trust.

> I prefer simplicity for my own investments, and I always aim to have at least 50% of my investments in index trackers. Over time, I might migrate more of my money into index trackers, but for now I get value from the risk management of active managers. A final point here: the active managers I have chosen are more prone to buy investments that I might naturally avoid, including commodities and new companies with high growth potential. So I am paying them to compensate for my weaknesses as an investor.

Example of a global balanced index-tracking portfolio

Here is an example of a global balanced index-tracking portfolio that should generate good capital growth over the long term:

- 70% in iShares MSCI ACWI ETF (global shares);
- 10% in iShares Global REIT ETF (global property);
- 10% in iShares Global Govt Bond UCITS ETF (global bonds);
- 5% in SPDR Gold Shares (gold ETF); and
- 5% in cash.

The gold and cash holdings are a form of portfolio insurance. I do not anticipate much growth from them, but they can be valuable in a major stock market crash. I call these two investments the 'shock absorbers'. It is important that you rebalance your portfolio consistently. That means you should aim to keep the percentage allocation as shown in the example. You can decide to review the balance annually (you do not need to do this too frequently) so that you catch any major imbalance in the portfolio before it becomes problematic. The reason you should not rebalance too frequently is that you will be charged transaction fees every time you rebalance, and stock markets are quite volatile, so smaller imbalances may resolve themselves within months.

CHAPTER 9

TWO SCENARIOS

There are generally two types of investors: people who want to retire with enough money for their lifetime, and people who are sure that they won't consume their capital over their lifetime. In this chapter, I profile these two general types of investors through two scenarios to discuss some of the factors they should consider when building a global portfolio.

Scenario A applies to most investors, namely those who want to retire with enough money for their lifetime. They are likely to spend the bulk of their money and leave only a little to their beneficiaries. Scenario B is for investors who will use only a portion of their capital over their lifetime. They must plan for the transfer of money to future generations and need to consider investments that differ from those a normal retiree would make. These are the investors who might need to invest in more complex structures such as a family trust.

Investor scenario A: Retire with enough money

There is a good chance that you will live for longer than retirees of the previous generation. All of us are living longer, and employers are encouraging people to retire earlier. This means the average person could be retired for 40-odd years.

Statistics tell us that in 1900, people in the USA lived to an average age of 47, while in 2020 the average age was 79. In Japan, the average lifespan in

1960 was 73 years, while in 2020 it was 85, so an average age of 90 cannot be far off. Fewer people are dying from disease and starvation, and improvements in healthcare have enabled people to live better-quality lives.

Ironically, increasing longevity could lead to economic difficulties in future. If most of the population is elderly and retired, there are fewer people to do the work of driving the economy. This means decreasing numbers of young people will have to support increasing numbers of ageing people. It also means that if you retire at age 65, you should plan to support yourself financially until at least age 90. I personally believe that healthy people with access to good healthcare should plan up until age 100 to be safe. If you subscribe to this view, there are some important considerations for your finances.

Factors to consider for your investments

The expected lifespan of an investment is the most important factor to consider when constructing any portfolio. You need to work out how long you should plan to invest your money before some or all of it will be required. It is important to remember that your biggest financial enemy during retirement is the rising cost of living. This is why you have to ensure that a portion of your money is invested in growth assets that have the best chance of growing faster than inflation over your lifetime.

Healthy people with enough capital should plan for their capital to last for a maximum of 40 years if they retire at age 65. This is called the 'time horizon' of the capital and informs how much risk you can take with your money. Your time horizon will be long enough to invest most of your money in shares so that you have the best chance of growth. However, you also need to balance the need for growth with the requirement for income from investments to fund your lifestyle costs. In my view, a good asset mix for someone in this position is 60% in shares, 15% in bonds, 15% in property investments and 10% in cash. This asset mix is a critical decision because it will determine how much capital growth you can achieve from your money over your lifetime. If you have too little in shares and property investments, your capital cannot beat inflation over time. Similarly, if you have 100% of your money in shares and property investments, you might find yourself in trouble during a big stock market crash. Shares can (and do) lose 50% of their value in a crash – and sometimes more.

If you are retired and living off your capital, it is important to limit your losses as much as possible. By reducing your shares and increasing your allocation to cash and bonds, it is possible to limit your losses while still generating some capital growth.

I have not distinguished between investments in your home country and global investments in this allocation. However, it is important to ensure that you have the correct asset mix irrespective of where your money lives. It is equally important to ensure that you maintain a consistent balance of assets over your lifetime. It is a good idea to rebalance the mix of your assets every year to ensure that your asset mix doesn't drift too much as markets rise or fall over time.

If you plan to live in your home country for the rest of your lifetime, you could consider allocating 50% to 75% of your assets to your home country, with the balance invested globally. Table 9.1 provides a clear way of deciding how much to invest in your home country. (Also see Chapter 7, where I indicate that your decisions about local and international investment exposure should be based on your financial goals and on where you plan to live once you retire.)

Table 9.1 Suggested allocations to local and international markets

Financial position	Amount allocated to home market	Amount allocated to overseas investments
Retiring with just enough money	75%	25%
Planning to leave some money to children	50%	50%
Planning to leave money to potential grandchildren	25%	75%

While your overall asset mix is key, you can be flexible when determining how to split your assets between local and overseas investments. One factor that is worth considering is tax treatment of interest and dividends. If your home country pays higher interest rates than overseas markets and you get some tax breaks on local interest, you could decide to have more of your cash at home while allocating more to shares in your international portfolio (if your local stock market is relatively small). The main point is to ensure that your overall allocation to shares is correct. Table 9.2 provides an example of an asset mix for someone planning to continue living in their home country who might leave some money to their children, and whose home country has a small economy with local interest rates much higher than global interest rates.

Read this table by adding the allocation to the local asset type to the international asset type to determine the total allocation. So, if you look at shares, 20% of your portfolio might be invested in local shares and a further 40% in international shares, for a total allocation to shares of 60%.

Table 9.2 Combined asset mix for a retiree

Asset type	Local investments	Overseas investments	Total allocation
Shares	20%	40%	60%
Property companies	5%	10%	15%
Bonds	10%	5%	15%
Cash	10%	0%	10%

If you are in a similar situation as the investor in this scenario, you will be planning to use most of your capital during your lifetime. Thus it will be important for you to consider how you will derive an income from your overseas investments. There might be some tax regulations in your home country to consider when doing this part of your planning. If tax is not relevant to the timing of your decisions, I prefer to keep things relatively simple. By this I mean that I would try to draw a portion of my overseas capital every six months to fund my living expenses. This can be managed on a flexible basis, as you might decide to draw more from local investments when your home currency is strong and more from international investments when your home currency is weak.

I have not included any commodities such as gold in the asset mix in this table. While I believe that gold is a good form of portfolio insurance (like the shock absorbers of your car), it will not help you generate an income to cover your lifestyle costs.

If you will be using most of your capital in your lifetime, it means that you do not need to consider complex estate-planning structures such as trusts. However, you should ensure that your overseas assets are held in a country where you will not be charged inheritance taxes on those assets when you pass away. This means considering countries such as Switzerland, Luxembourg, Ireland or the Channel Islands for overseas investments. It is of vital importance to confirm what documentation these countries will require in the event of your death. This includes ascertaining whether you will need a will in that country for your overseas investments or whether the will from your home country is sufficient.

Understanding the impact of economic and market conditions

One of the difficult aspects of retirement planning is that you need to make assumptions about how much capital growth you will need every year for the remainder of your life. The best growth assets are investments in shares and property companies. You may remember from Chapter 6, Table 6.2, that over many decades, international shares and property companies have grown by around 3% to 6% per year above inflation, but this growth may have been either much lower or much higher at times.

When determining how much growth to expect from your overseas assets, you have to focus on long-term returns. Do not get sucked into thinking about the recent performance of these assets when doing your calculations. Recent performance is nearly worthless in any forecast about future growth. Sticking to your long-term asset mix is very important when markets are rocky and everyone is pessimistic. It is best to avoid making big changes in times of market volatility, as this is likely to prevent years of hardship later.

How much capital do you need?

At the start of this book, I referenced the Bengen rule, also known as the 4% rule. This rule of thumb is helpful when determining how much capital you will need once you stop working for a living. In Chapter 2 I mentioned that you will need a capital amount of $300 000 for every $1 000 worth of monthly expenses to be sure that you can continue living a sustainable life. If you plan to spend $4 000 per month in today's value once you are no longer working, then you will need $1.2 million in capital in today's value to stop working. Depending on where you live, these amounts might vary slightly, but they are based on the rule of spending 4% of your investment money every year. In my experience, this is a great guide for investors across the globe. If you have a well-diversified global portfolio, relying on 4% of your investments for income will work in most circumstances.

What if you have not saved enough for retirement?

If you have not saved enough for retirement, the temptation is to aim for more capital growth and take on more risk at a stage when you are drawing income from your capital. But, in this instance, what you really need to do is to take less risk.

The best solution for insufficient retirement capital is to reduce your lifestyle costs – and that may mean having to make a complete lifestyle change. Moving to a small town or a lower-cost country can save you a fair amount, because the costs of food, security, insurance and so on are likely to be lower. Property values and taxes tend to be much higher in cities too, especially in developed economies. There are some countries that offer a great lifestyle at a relatively affordable cost of living. There are some great expat surveys that are published annually to show which countries offer the best combination of low cost of living, great quality of life, and expat-friendly taxes and incentives.

Plan together

Many people really struggle in their first few years of retirement. It is wise not to simply assume that your partner has the same ideas about retirement as you do – you must discuss it. If possible, try to ensure that both of you retire at approximately the same time.

If only one person has been earning an income, the situation can be even more complicated at retirement. The person who spent most of their time at home has a routine and a life that is independent of their partner's. When that partner suddenly spends every day at home, it can be disruptive to both. The Covid-19 pandemic has led to many people working from home for at least some time. This had many couples experiencing a forced experiment of the implications of sharing their home seven days a week instead of on weekends only. This experience will hopefully prompt them to plan ahead for their life in retirement.

Planning for death

It is uncomfortable to think about this matter, but you should also start planning for death. If you are in a relationship, often one partner does most of the money planning. This can be problematic. Both partners in a relationship need to understand how their joint finances work and how their investments are structured, and they need to agree on their investment strategy.

Both partners should meet with their financial planner (if they have one) and both need to be comfortable with this person. Financial planning is a relationship between three parties, and it is important to remember that if one partner passes away, the other will have to deal with the financial planner from then onwards.

Furthermore, it is very important to keep your will updated and to review this important document every two to three years. Appoint a professional to assist with this, as legal issues around inheritance taxes and probate processes can be tricky.

Downscaling and the family home

If you are planning to scale down by moving from a larger family home to something smaller and more appropriate at retirement, try to choose your new home far in advance. It becomes progressively more difficult to make decisions about downscaling when you reach your late 70s or early 80s. You should also factor in considerations such as frail care and plan for this eventuality as early as possible. It is very traumatic for everyone if you need to scramble for a suitable frail-care solution for a loved one who has developed a medical issue and requires constant care.

If you have children, it is important to discuss your plans with them. Many retirees make plans around their children, especially when choosing where to live, only to discover that their children are planning to move to a different city or country. It is far better if you plan your ideal retirement around your own requirements instead. It is imperative to have a strong social network when you are no longer working; research has shown that this is a vital aspect of mental wellbeing. Loneliness and social isolation can become real problems in retirement, but they can be avoided through better planning.

If you want to leave a family property to your adult children, it is worth discussing this plan with those who will inherit the property. Importantly, they need to start taking responsibility for the management and maintenance of this property while you are still alive. Many parents spend huge amounts of time and money maintaining a property 'for the children', and their children then sell the property once the parents have passed away.

Investor scenario B: Intergenerational wealth

All the factors discussed in scenario A might apply to wealthy families too. But wealthy families have some additional factors to consider.

When you are planning to leave money to future generations, your investment planning becomes a bit more complex because there are multiple investment time horizons to consider. In addition, the transfer of money from one generation to another requires estate planning that might involve trusts or companies or both, with potential tax consequences in multiple countries. Lastly, if there is a family business (including farming operations), your succession planning must include decisions about the ownership of the business and whether this conveys any rights to the owners to work in the business and/or manage it in future. Large farms or businesses are complex entities. The mere fact that people inherit ownership of a complex entity doesn't mean they should work in that entity. More importantly, they might not be the right people to manage or lead this entity into the future.

Different generations mean different time horizons

When I consult with wealthy families, I often suggest that they divide their assets into different portions, because each generation will have different objectives for their money. Families might also want to plan for future generations who have not been conceived yet. To start, I always aim to identify a portion of capital that is solely used to fund the lifestyle costs of the oldest generation for the remainder of their lives. This capital must provide a monthly income while continuing to grow fast enough to match or beat inflation. This portion can be managed in a very similar way to that of other retirees. This is called the nest egg capital.

Once I have helped the family identify the nest egg capital, we can consider how the balance of the capital should be allocated and invested. If there is only sufficient capital to fund the next generation, we consider a time horizon of 40 to 80 years for this portion, depending on the ages of the children. This time horizon allows us to invest a large portion of the capital in high-growth assets such as shares and property companies, and a much smaller amount in cash and bonds, because there is no requirement to generate an income for several years.

If there is sufficient capital to fund three or more generations in the family, the time horizon extends beyond a hundred years. Clearly, it is impossible to forecast investment outcomes that far ahead with any confidence. That means an investment portfolio should be highly diversified, with a large range of asset types invested in many different countries. I am very reluctant to recommend too much of the capital being allocated to any single investment. The first priority for this money should be protection from permanent loss of capital. The second priority is to ensure capital growth at a faster rate than inflation. The final priority is to generate long-term sustainable capital growth without forgoing the first two priorities.

The lengthy time horizon does allow for a portion of the capital to be invested in more specialised investments, such as private equity, venture capital or even new asset types such as cryptocurrencies. The important consideration here is that the portion of money allocated to these types of investments should be much smaller than the portion allocated to index-tracking funds or large diversified portfolios of shares. In some instances, the family might have its own mutual funds or investment companies to ensure efficient management of the capital. To balance the higher-growth (and higher-risk) investments, this type of portfolio needs to have a portion allocated to very conservative assets too. These might include physical gold and a range of property assets in different developed countries. The purpose of the property assets is to protect against inflation and unforeseen market events that might occur in 50 or 100 years' time. Investors should buy in developed countries with a history of strong legal protection for investor rights and a stable political environment. I especially like to suggest farmland and coastal properties in developed countries as a hedge against the unknown.

Legal structures such as trusts and companies will play an important role in the transfer of wealth to future generations. Trusts can be very effective if you want to ensure that your money moves from you to your children in a controlled way. They are particularly valuable if your children are very young or if you have concerns about their ability to deal with money in the future. Such circumstances include children or other dependants with mental health issues, disabilities or substance-abuse problems. In addition, families might want to limit the financial impact of marriages or divorces on the capital that they wish to preserve for future generations. When developing legal structures for trusts, it is important to cater for the fact that future generations will have diverging priorities and might live in different countries. Sufficient planning can ensure that family trusts are separated over time to be replaced by new trusts that cater to new family groupings without changing the overall purpose of the capital.

The family constitution

Many of the wealthiest families in the world have a family constitution that outlines the principles governing how the family will transfer wealth to future generations. This might include the family's priorities on social causes, philanthropy and other general investment principles.

Such a constitution should include the responsibilities of each family member and what they need to do to receive benefits from the family assets. For example, some families require all family members to receive a minimum standard of education and commit a specific amount of time to charities before they receive financial benefits. While most of these families are very private, there is visible evidence of a family constitution in some aristocratic families. The constitution might include an obligation to attend certain schools, do a minimum period of national service, spend a certain number of hours every year working in charities, and so on. Family members are all aware of their responsibilities and these are generally enforced by independent trustees rather than direct family members. The trustees are often a combination of designated family members and independent professionals.

I suggest that wealthy families take responsibility for the financial education of their children. The founders of wealthy families often neglect this responsibility as they are busy building the family fortune. They forget to educate the next generation on investments, family responsibilities and intergenerational planning. This means the first generation to inherit money is often unprepared for the responsibility of wealth, and this can lead to financial disaster.

Family businesses and family farms

It makes sense to address family farms and family businesses together as a topic, because they are often the foundation of wealth for future generations. They are also frequently the cause of major conflict within families. When a big business or farm is the source of wealth, it is important to realise that the management of this asset needs to be separated from its ownership. In the case of a farm, it is not practical to continually divide a farm into smaller units for future generations to inherit. A better solution is for the family to remain owners of the farm (through a trust), and for the person who is managing the farm to be a qualified and experienced family member or professional manager. The family or their representatives can then form part of the board of directors, together with additional independent professional directors. It will be the board's responsibility to appoint and monitor the management of the company or farm. This type of structure has been effectively implemented with the ownership of Walmart by the Walton family. While the family (through their legal structures) own a large share of Walmart, they are not involved in the daily management of the company. There are many options to explore with this type of structure; for example, it is possible to offer family members the option of working in the family business provided they obtain the necessary qualifications and compete on an equal footing with non-family members. I am not a proponent of arrangements that guarantee family members senior management roles in a large business or farm, as this can lead to bad outcomes if these family members are not qualified for their roles. Nepotism within any large commercial enterprise can be very destructive to the enterprise and this will have negative financial consequences for all family members, including those who are not working in the business.

I believe that some careful planning for the future and some open conversations within families can save a lot of heartache and financial difficulty in the future. Parents should not avoid conversations with their children about money or how it should be transferred to future generations, even if these are awkward or uncomfortable topics to discuss. If parents do not plan properly and fail to communicate their plans with the next generation, this can result in financial ruin for their children or grandchildren. If there is a family business or family farm, the need for succession planning and for managing these enterprises is critical, and sentiment or tradition might lead to terrible outcomes. Should you find yourself in this position and be unable to start the succession-planning process yourself, I advise you to appoint trusted professionals to assist you. Your children and grandchildren will be grateful!

CHAPTER 10

WHY BUY RESIDENTIAL PROPERTY?

From the time we are very young, we are told that owning property is a good idea – that we should pay our own mortgage rather than pay off the mortgage for some landlord. And so, when we start work, we duly buy a home and take on the financial burden of a mortgage. This is how most of us embark on our lifelong property odyssey because our first property purchase is rarely the last one! When we require more space in future, for partners and children, we need to spend more on a bigger house with a larger mortgage. This process carries on until we retire and decide to look for a smaller home – hopefully, this time without the need for a mortgage. Many of us keep doing something simply because our parents or society did the same in the past. This social pressure can be quite subtle, but it is very powerful and can cause people to live a compromised lifestyle merely because they are trying to satisfy other people's expectations of them. But I believe there is an alternative view to property ownership.

Do not buy that house!

Since the 1960s, in most countries around the world, investments in shares have grown in value more than three times faster than house prices. If you judge the two as pure investments, it makes sense to invest all your money in shares and rather pay rent for your home. Investing the difference between affordable rent and home ownership costs can help you achieve financial freedom far sooner than those who buy their homes. This is because home ownership includes unproductive costs like transaction fees and property taxes that add no value to the price of the home.

Most studies on property ownership show that it is usually better to rent a home instead of buying one. This is especially true if you plan to buy a new, larger home every three to five years. The transaction costs associated with buying and selling a residential property every few years are so high that they can destroy any potential capital growth you might have earned from the property price growth.

In addition to property transaction costs, there are other costs of home ownership to consider. For example, home ownership means maintenance and insurance costs you do not pay as a renter, and you will have to pay property taxes in most countries. Transaction costs and property taxes are sunk costs that add no value to the property. I believe that a disciplined saver who pays sensible rent over a lifetime can generally achieve financial freedom more quickly than someone who buys a home. It is worth considering some factual market data to explain my view.

Property as an investment

If we were to consider residential property as a 'pure' investment, we should compare it to other pure investments such as shares and bonds. In Table 10.1 I compare the long-term performance of global shares, global property companies (a type of share), global bonds, cash, and global residential property prices. It is important to note that it is very difficult to get accurate long-term residential property prices, so I considered different studies from countries around the world to show a fair range of returns from residential property. Critically, I have not factored in the cost of buying, maintaining or selling any of the asset types in the table. However, the costs associated with residential property are far higher than those of other asset types.

Table 10.1 Global growth of main asset types above inflation compared to residential property

Asset type	Long-term real growth per year
Global shares	5.6%
Global property companies	3.6%
Global bonds	1.5%
Cash (USA interest rates)	1.2%
Global residential property	0.5% to 1.1%

Source: Nedgroup Investments, Case-Shiller, Eichholtz (author's analysis)

From the table we see that the best-performing investment (asset class) is the share market. Over the long term it has beaten inflation by 5.6% per year, while residential property ranks fifth, outperforming inflation by only 0.5% to 1.1% per year. If this seems too low to you, consider the results of a brilliant study completed in 1994 by Piet Eichholtz, titled 'A Long Run House Price Index: The Herengracht Index, 1628–1973'. This study measured the growth of property prices in the Herengracht district of Amsterdam. It shows that over nearly 400 years, real house-price growth has averaged only 0.5% per annum over the entire period. The results are fairly consistent over each century too, with the lowest real growth of negative 0.2% per annum occurring in the 18th and 20th centuries, and the highest real growth of 1.3% per annum occurring in the 17th century.

Eichholtz's study is valuable in that it focuses on one specific area in which the houses have not changed in size (it is a historical site). Also, the area has always been considered a prime residential area, so performance has not been affected by urban decay. What the study shows is that residential property tracks inflation over the long term. In other words, one should not expect an investment in a home to beat inflation by a significant amount. This is especially true if you factor in the costs associated with home ownership.

One of the major costs is a mortgage or home loan. The average mortgage interest rate over certain periods has been higher than the nominal growth on property (that is, before inflation). This means that investors in residential property actually pay more in interest than they gain in growth on the value of the property. That is why I believe that mortgaged residential property is a poor investment over the very long term.

Mortgage interest is not the only cost of owning a home. There are also the initial costs of buying the home. These vary depending on the country of purchase, but they usually include legal costs, property taxes and banking fees. You might also need to pay a fee to estate agents when you buy or sell your home. Once you have taken ownership of the property, you will need to factor in maintenance costs and ongoing property taxes.

You might still not be convinced that residential property is a poorly performing asset and believe it is a low-risk investment. However, there are some significant risks to consider. These include concentration and liquidity risks. Concentration risk means having too much of your capital exposed to one investment (having too many eggs in one basket), while liquidity risk refers to the ability to sell an investment quickly.

Perhaps you are disciplined with your mortgage repayments and can pay off the cost of your home sooner than the mortgage term. However, it is important to consider the value of the money you have tied up in your home. This money is 'dead' capital because it is not working for you. If you have the equivalent of $500 000 invested in your home, consider how much you would pay to rent a similar property. Then compare this cost to the growth that your $500 000 could have achieved from a global portfolio of shares over the long term. In most instances, it would have made sense to rent a property and use the income from a $500 000 global investment to fund the rental cost.

Property investing is actually a business

I have known many people who have built significant asset values by investing in residential property. I have also known many people who have made fortunes on the share market. Both groups have turned their investing into a business — that is, they have become professional investors. But for someone working in a different career, say, a medical specialist who doesn't have time to be a professional share investor, it would make far more sense to invest in an ETF or mutual fund for 15 years. I believe the same applies to residential property investors.

The time, effort and expertise required to be a property investor is significant. You cannot simply buy a rental house and forget about it for 15 years. You must ensure that you have tenants, the property needs to be maintained, and you need to pay the relevant taxes. You will also have to monitor the neighbourhood around the house. Over 15 years it is likely that the area will change – it either becomes more desirable or it declines.

Some estate agents offer a 'rental management' service, whereby they find you tenants and manage your property for you. You need to be very careful before using such a service; some estate agents will promise a lot, charge a fortune and do very little. From painful personal experience I can tell you that some agents do not scrutinise the tenants properly and rarely take any real interest in maintaining your property. Over the long term, if you want to make money from rental properties, you will need to manage the properties yourself or hire a very reliable person to manage them for you.

Once you are doing active work on your investments regularly, you are no longer a passive investor but an entrepreneur running a business, which happens to be property investing. On that basis, you could make substantial money because you will spend significantly more time on your investments. This is an important difference, as most people are passive investors and cannot actively work on their investments while pursuing their careers.

Do buy that house!

I concede that you cannot make the decision to buy a home on investment performance alone. There are other factors to consider around home ownership too, including the emotional value of owning your own castle or nest. After all, even Warren Buffett owns his own home, and he is one of the greatest share investors of all time. There are some very real non-investment benefits to home ownership, for example if you need to obtain permanent residence or citizenship in another country. Through a Golden Visa programme, you can buy the right to become a permanent resident or even a citizen of another country by purchasing a property. The regulations of the

Golden Visa programme will specify certain conditions to the property purchase, and the properties in question might be significantly more expensive than comparable properties in the same area. These programmes can be very attractive as a form of insurance against political or economic instability in your home country. In addition, there might be potential tax savings if you are planning to retire and your home country is a high-tax country. Finally, there are people who wish to move to a country where they can have a high standard of living at a lower cost than in their home country.

I am not opposed to Golden Visa programmes per se. However, in my view they are often sold to people under false pretences. For example, unscrupulous salespeople create the impression that these programmes are only available for a limited time, while many countries have offered them for decades. But some are very expensive and do not guarantee citizenship or permanent residence. I prefer the approach of building a large overseas investment that can be used if and when needed to relocate to another country one day.

So, I believe it makes sense to own your home if you want to live in the same property for more than 10 years and preferably for decades. This is because you will be limiting your property transaction costs and spreading them out over many years. Also, the cost of rent over a long period will escalate with inflation, and eventually your rental amount will become substantially higher than the cost of maintenance and other costs associated with property ownership. Finally, there is a real lifestyle benefit to having a fixed home without the emotional upheaval of moving and the associated costs of relocating to a new property.

Another good reason to buy your home relates to those who are financially less disciplined. Many people are not good at saving their money over the long term. They find it far too easy to sell their investments to buy a new car, or they blow the money on a dream holiday. If you are not a disciplined saver, it might make sense to buy a home. If the fear of losing your home isn't enough to force you to pay your mortgage every month, nothing will! And this discipline will at least ensure that you have one paid-off asset on retirement.

Some financial pundits point out that it is usually quite easy to borrow money from a bank to buy a house if you are in a reasonable financial position. They argue that most people find it easier to borrow money to buy a house than for any other purpose, especially if they earn a good salary. The theory is that if they are disciplined in paying off their mortgage quickly, they can use the house as an asset to borrow money to buy other investments. I am not necessarily advocating this, because it is a very risky way to make money, but it is possible and could be another benefit of owning a residential property.

When is a good time to buy property?

The best time to buy a residential property is when the rental cost is more than the monthly bond repayment on the same type of property. This doesn't happen often, and when it does you should take advantage, because house prices are bound to increase substantially.

Unfortunately, there is no magic financial model that can protect you from your own financial frailties, so rather be honest with yourself before making serious financial decisions. There are also important lifestyle issues that cannot be factored into a financial model.

All property investments are heavily influenced by interest rates. When interest rates fall substantially, property prices usually increase a great deal. Similarly, when interest rates increase, property prices tend to stagnate or decline.

A country's economic growth rate has a major influence on property investments, although the effects of this influence are often delayed. If the economy grows substantially, property prices tend to rise. Generally, however, there are major lag times between economic growth and the resulting price appreciation. Similarly, the economy could stagnate, and property might continue to rise in price for a few years before prices stall.

Most large properties or developments are valued according to the level of income they generate rather than the actual value of the land or the building. Any factors that hamper rental income are likely to have a direct impact on the prices of commercial and industrial properties. Other factors such as population growth, electricity costs, the political environment, legislation changes, crime and sentiment will also affect property prices.

Lastly, major demographic trends within a country will drive property prices significantly. If people start to move out of cities in search of more spacious homes in the countryside, as might happen after the pandemic, this could lead to declining prices in cities and rising prices in smaller country towns.

CHAPTER 11

OVERVIEW OF INVESTMENT TERMS

So far, we have looked at different types of investments and how you can put them together to create your own unique mix of assets to suit your long-term financial objectives. In this chapter, I provide easy-to-refer-to explanations of the different investment terms covered in this book.

Bonds

A bond is a debt investment where an investor loans money to an entity (usually a corporate or government entity) that borrows the money for a defined period at a fixed interest rate. Bonds are used by companies, municipalities, states and governments to finance a variety of projects and activities.

Just as your home loan is also referred to as a bond – because you owe money to the bank over a fixed term – a bond is an investment in which you, the investor, lend money to either a company or a government entity for a defined period at a fixed interest rate.

Interest on bonds is usually paid every six months, and the interest rate is mainly determined by two criteria: the credit quality of the entity that issues the bond, and the bond's lifespan, which can extend for decades.

The major difference between bonds and shares is that shareholders own a part of the company, while a bondholder is simply owed money by the company or government entity. Shares have an indefinite lifespan, while bonds have a defined lifespan.

Bonds that are issued by financially sound governments or corporates can be a great source of income for retirees. Most bonds will track or even slightly outperform inflation with the income they pay to investors. Because bonds yield returns in a completely different way to shares, they represent a diversifying element in any portfolio.

Your best way to buy bonds is via a mutual fund or an ETF.

Cryptocurrencies (Bitcoin & co.)

In my rather simplistic understanding, I think of cryptocurrencies (or cryptos) as a new way of transacting. A major advantage of cryptos is that they use a recordkeeping technology (called blockchain) that is very hard to forge or corrupt.

In addition, there is the potential for cryptos to be operated and valued by millions of people worldwide rather than by one government or central bank. I like the potential applications of blockchain for millions of businesses around the world, not only for cryptocurrencies. For example, large retailers can track the movement of their goods from the time the goods are made by the supplier to the time they are sold in a specific shop. It should even be possible to track the origin of the fruit you buy in a food store. This could be a powerful tool for retailers and consumers alike.

My main concern with Bitcoin and most other cryptos is their volatility. Prices move in massive swings almost daily, and therefore it is hard to use them to buy things, especially if your transaction will take place over a few days, such as when you buy something from overseas.

I think cryptos are also in danger of being regulated out of existence by governments around the world. It is a weakness of cryptos that owners of the assets can remain anonymous, and this creates the opportunity for terrorists, organised criminals and corrupt politicians to hide their ill-gotten gains. The crypto market is evolving rapidly, and I would not be surprised to see cryptos becoming a viable competitor to gold as a store of wealth that is delinked from stock markets, currencies and other asset types.

Developed markets

A developed market typically occurs in developed economies, which are characterised by a relatively high level of income per person and a secure political environment. Common characteristics of developed economies are that they are usually politically and economically stable, that their legal system is well structured, and that citizens, the state and business have good legal protection. Citizens have access to social support (such as healthcare, education and social welfare). While developed economies can be quite small, some, like the USA, are enormous.

Dividends

When a company makes a profit, it might decide to pay some of that profit to the owners of the company (its shareholders). The payment to shareholders is called a dividend, and the amount paid to each shareholder is determined by the number of shares each one holds. Dividends are usually paid in cash, but sometimes shareholders are offered shares to the same value as the cash instead. Dividends can attract tax, but the taxes are usually more tax-efficient than interest or rental income. Over time, your dividends can increase in value if the company does well and profits go up.

Dow Jones, S&P 500 and Nasdaq

The USA still represents more than 55% of the world's stock market value. Global investors monitor this market closely, as the upward or downward movement of stock markets worldwide is affected by the US market in the short term. The most well-known are the Dow Jones, S&P 500 and Nasdaq indices. The S&P 500 tracks the 500 largest companies listed on the US stock exchanges, the Dow Jones Industrial Average consists of 30 large listed US shares, and the Nasdaq tracks most of the companies listed on the Nasdaq stock exchange. I generally advise clients to avoid ETFs that track the Dow Jones and rather consider the S&P 500. The Nasdaq is often described as the tech index, and many investors who want to monitor the tech sector focus exclusively on the Nasdaq rather than the S&P 500 or Dow Jones. But most big tech companies are also represented in the S&P 500, which is why I prefer it over the Nasdaq for diversification reasons. For investors who only want to buy one globally diversified investment, I would advise an ETF tracking the MSCI ACWI (see 'World market indices' at the end of this chapter).

Emerging markets

Emerging market economies share some characteristics with developed markets, but they tend to be situated in countries that have large and growing populations and a fast-growing economy. These markets are generally riskier and more volatile than those in a developed economy, but they can offer more opportunities for capital growth. Historically, emerging market economies were smaller than developed economies, but this has changed over time. For example, many investors still classify China as an emerging market, although it is in a race with the USA to be the largest economy in the world.

Exchange traded funds (ETFs)

ETFs are traded on the stock market like ordinary shares, but they consist of a basket of investments, including shares, bonds and properties. Investments in ETFs generally attract very low ongoing fees and no upfront fees, which makes them ideal for private investors who want to invest through large lump sums or smaller monthly amounts.

Most ETFs are based on an index, or a selection of shares representing a particular market as a whole or a particular market sector. For example, one of the biggest ETFs in the world is the SPDR S&P 500 ETF Trust, which tracks the 500 largest companies listed on stock exchanges in the USA. Instead of buying shares in each of these 500 companies individually, you buy one ETF that owns shares in all of them.

I am a big fan of indexed ETFs. A low-cost ETF that owns a diversified selection of shares is the best option for anyone with limited resources but who can afford to put a regular amount of money each month into an investment. ETFs are usually much cheaper than life assurance company investments and are often cheaper than mutual funds too.

An increasing number of ETFs and other indexed products are being launched, and many are becoming more exotic and difficult to understand. I advise inexperienced investors to stick to the KIS principle with ETFs: keep it simple! It is the nature of product providers to try to sell 'newer and better' products all the time in an effort to differentiate themselves and accumulate more assets from investors. But the fact that they need to sell these products doesn't mean that you should buy them.

Many different companies offer ETFs. As a rule, I like to buy ETFs that already have a large asset base because they can achieve some economies of scale with reduced transaction charges and fewer additional costs. When selecting ETFs for your global portfolio, remember that the country where the ETF is listed is critical to avoid unnecessary taxes.

Fixed deposits

A fixed deposit is a kind of savings account that usually pays a fixed rate of interest for a fixed period. As the name suggests, you make a deposit for a fixed period so that the money can earn a guaranteed amount of interest until the maturity date arrives.

Funds placed in a fixed deposit account cannot be withdrawn prior to maturity, although some banks offer slight variations on this rule: sometimes the funds can be withdrawn if you give advance notice, but you might incur a penalty for this.

Fixed deposits are relatively safe investments when provided by financial institutions such as banks, savings and loan corporations, and credit unions that are properly registered and regulated. Because the bank guarantees your interest rate and term, there will be no surprises with this type of investment.

However, fixed deposits are not my favourite investments. Although they are low risk, they also yield low returns. So you should use them only if you need to keep your money in cash for a specific purpose. I also dislike long-term fixed deposits (that is, longer than three years), as these seldom give better-than-inflation returns and you can get better growth from other low-risk investments.

Hedge funds

Hedge funds are investments that pool together money from various investors. This money is then invested in a variety of investments and in many different strategies. This can include the use of borrowing or more exotic instruments such as derivatives. The original purpose of hedge funds was to reduce the risk of portfolios (literally to hedge your bets), but their purpose has changed over time. Some hedge funds can be extremely risky, as they aim to deliver large returns for investors. I do not like hedge funds, because they usually attract very high fees, the investment strategies are complex, and they are not transparent to outside investors.

Home loans

A home loan, mortgage or bond is a loan from a bank or other financial institution to assist people in buying their own homes. The bank will lend you money to buy a house conditional on your credit record, your ability to afford the repayments, and finding sufficient value in the home in question to secure the loan. Interest is payable on your home loan. The home loan amount is usually loaned over a set period, typically between 15 and 30 years, and you pay back an instalment on that loan every month for the full period of the loan.

Provided your monthly repayments are affordable, this is the only way most people can afford to buy their homes. Unfortunately, many people buy homes that are too expensive, and they have to use all their spare income to repay their mortgage when they should also be investing some of their money for their retirement. Be sure to factor in additional costs – rates, insurance, maintenance costs and so on – when you purchase a home.

By paying extra money into your bond each month, you can reduce the amount of interest you pay over the period of the home loan. This will bring down the repayment amount. A good tip is to always try to pay off your mortgage within 10 to 15 years.

If you are financially disciplined, your home loan can be a source of low-cost finance for other assets. Some people use their home loan as a credit facility to buy a car or purchase growth assets such as shares. This can be a very efficient way of using debt at good interest rates. Be cautious, though: doing so can make it very easy to fall into an even bigger debt trap.

Index investing

Index investors try to get the same return as that generated by a specific index. Most of these indices are based on shares, bonds or listed property. The most quoted index in the world is the S&P 500 index, which tracks the 500 largest companies listed on stock exchanges in the USA. The index is usually quoted as a number, for example 'the S&P 500 reached 4 122'. This number is the 'value' of all the shares on the stock market but is meaningful only in that it explains whether the stock market has gone up or down over a specific period (over one day, one week, one month, one year and so on).

History has proven that it is very difficult for most investors to beat an index over long periods. When you invest in a fund or other product that aims to beat an index, there are management costs, transaction costs and other charges that must be recouped regularly. Moreover, most investors are simply wrong in their investment decisions more often than they are right.

Seven out of every ten mutual funds in the world have not been able to beat their index over 10-year periods. A handful of great money managers have beaten the index over the long term (Warren Buffett is one of them), but they are few and far between, and we tend to find out about them only after they have peaked as investors.

By far the best decision that new investors can make is to invest in low-cost indexed investments. Over the long term, you will be better off than most fund managers. There is little need for you to do anything or manage anything, as the investment is passive in nature. However, you should be prepared to leave your money in the index for at least seven to ten years without making changes.

Inheritance tax, situs, estate tax or death duty

When deciding on overseas investments, it is critical to find out about the taxes that might be charged during your lifetime and when you pass away. Many investors are attracted to destinations such as the USA or the UK when they look for a home for their overseas investments. Unfortunately, both the UK and the USA charge some form of tax when a non-resident investor passes away while owning assets in those countries. In the USA, a non-resident who passes away while owning shares listed in the USA might have to pay estate tax of 40% on any investments worth more than $60 000. The UK will similarly charge a 40% inheritance tax when non-residents have UK assets worth more than GBP325 000. This can be a nasty surprise for those who inherit your assets. There are some well-regulated, safe countries that do not levy such taxes on non-residents.

Investment companies or investment trusts

Specialised investment companies, also known as investment trusts, are listed on a stock exchange and traded in the same way as any normal share with the aim of managing portfolios of investments for shareholders. These are mainly designed for private investors who want to access high-quality investments that might not be accessible for direct investment. Because investment companies are listed on a stock exchange, they are well regulated and relatively transparent. Through these, investors have access to a wide range of investments, including private companies. Some investment companies are very specialised and invest only in certain sectors of the stock market or in certain geographic areas. Others are more diversified and flexible in their investment approach.

Money market accounts

A money market account is an account at a bank that pays a higher interest rate than the other savings vehicles that banks usually offer. In exchange, you have to keep a fairly high minimum balance in the account. Also, there are restrictions on how many transactions you can make through the account per month. A money market account is thus a savings account with terms and conditions attached, but better interest rates.

The interest rates for money market accounts are usually higher than for other very low-risk investments, and there are no obligations to invest your money for fixed periods. Because the funds are readily available, money market accounts are a good choice for an emergency cash fund. But as with all cash investments, they are not a good place to keep your money for the long term. However, the interest you earn in a money market account is likely to beat inflation over time.

Mutual funds

Mutual funds are also known as collective investment schemes (CISs) or undertakings for the collective investment in transferable securities (UCITSs). Mutual funds are well-regulated investments and popular among investors. They are open-ended: they have no set size limit or any limits to the number of investors. They are operated by an investment company with a separate institution acting as custodian of the assets of the fund. Each investor in the mutual fund is called a unit holder, and the investors are the only owners of the mutual fund. A wide range of mutual funds is available, representing a variety of assets: shares, bonds, property, cash, gold and indexed investments.

Because mutual funds are transparent, you can find out exactly how much money you have invested in the fund and how it is invested every day. There are some very good low-cost, index-tracking mutual funds that are ideal for most investors. Mutual funds in general are by far my preferred investment vehicle for all types of individual investors.

However, be aware that some mutual funds are ridiculously expensive. Unscrupulous asset managers may charge unfair performance fees to enrich themselves at the cost of their clients. Some mutual funds also invest in other mutual funds – an investment strategy called a fund of funds (FOF) – and their costs can also be exorbitant.

Pension plans or retirement funds

Pension plans or retirement funds are highly regulated investments that are governed by specific laws that are unique to each country. Often there is a tax benefit to investing in a retirement fund. However, there might be some restrictions on how and when you can access the money invested in these funds. Pension plans in one country might not be recognised as such in other countries. These include structures such as overseas pension schemes. I advise clients to be careful of investing in these without proper tax advice.

Property companies and real estate investment trusts (REITs)

Throughout this book I have referred to property companies – companies whose shares are traded on the stock exchange. You can invest in these in the form of property companies or REITs. REITs generally own a variety of office blocks, industrial buildings, warehouses, shopping malls and even residential properties.

REITs should be an investment of choice for investors who prefer property to normal shares. I often recommend investments in property companies in conjunction with bonds to investors who require inflation-beating income and diversification.

Property companies are very sensitive to interest-rate fluctuations: prices rise when interest rates are low. So low interest rates can cause share-price bubbles. There is also a risk that investment managers might borrow too much at the wrong time and place the company in jeopardy. Larger property companies generally represent less of a risk.

Savings accounts

A savings account is the simplest way to save, apart from putting your money in a piggy bank or hiding it under the mattress – neither of which will earn you any interest. A savings account is a simple deposit held at a bank or other financial institution and usually provides a modest interest rate. It is easy to withdraw cash from savings accounts, so these can be useful to hold funds that you do not need for daily expenses. A money market account or money market mutual fund is usually a better choice, because the interest rates are likely to be better than what a savings account offers.

Shares

A share represents the smallest unit of ownership in a company. You can own shares in private companies and in companies that trade on the stock market. Investors often refer to shares as equities, as these two terms are interchangeable.

When a company initially lists its shares on the stock market, it sells shares to investors as a way of raising money (or capital). The income that a shareholder earns from owning a share is called a dividend. Companies are not obliged to pay dividends, but most of the larger, established listed companies do pay dividends to shareholders when profits allow, usually on a six-monthly basis.

If you want to buy or sell shares in a private company, you will need to arrange your own transaction, whereas the trading of shares in a listed company is done on the stock exchange via a stockbroker. Most private investors will own shares through a mutual fund, retirement fund or ETF.

Shares are volatile (their prices go up and down), because they are subject to the vagaries of the emotional tide that affects investors around the world. Many fortunes have been created and destroyed by investors who think they can predict the market. Uninformed or lax investors who do not do their homework when buying individual shares are likely to lose money.

All investors should have a portion of their long-term investments in shares (at least 35%, but up to a maximum of 100% if you are under 30 years old). You do not need to invest in shares directly: ETFs and mutual funds are great vehicles for investing in shares because these allow you to diversify your investment from the outset. Keep in mind that over the long term, more than 40% of the return generated by shares on the stock market is the re-investment of dividends. If you do not reinvest your dividends, you will severely limit your potential capital growth.

Stock exchange or stock market

A stock market or stock exchange is where shares in public companies, ETFs and bonds are bought and sold. Historically, stock exchanges were only for shares in public companies, but this has changed over time. Nowadays, many ETFs, bonds and other types of investments can be traded on a stock exchange. Most stock exchanges are highly regulated, and all transactions are concluded electronically. Investors trade their shares online via a stockbroker.

Tax-efficient investments

When I decide to select an investment, tax is one of my last considerations. I will always default to an investment that delivers good returns, even if they are taxable. In my experience, complex products designed to avoid tax rarely outperform good taxable investments, even on an after-tax basis. One of the main exceptions to this rule are regulated pension or retirement funds. These may offer great returns to investors who are happy to remain in their home country.

Trusts

Trusts originated in the time of the Crusades in the 12th and 13th centuries, when English knights left their homes to fight abroad. These Crusades usually lasted many years, and there was no certainty that the knight would return. A knight therefore left his assets to someone he trusted and who was expected to manage his estate (mainly farms) for the benefit of the knight and his family.

Today, a trust is an arrangement whereby property is held by one party (the trustee) for the benefit of another (the beneficiary). A trust can be created either while you are alive or at the time of your death, if this is stipulated in your will.

If you place money in a trust, you are legally giving the money to a new 'person', and therefore you have no right to the money thereafter unless you are a beneficiary of the trust. The trustees run the trust and manage its affairs according to a written document, called a trust deed, which stipulates how the money should be managed and who should benefit from it. Trust law is complex, so you need to ensure that your trust is correctly structured and is created for the right reasons.

> ### REASONS FOR CREATING A TRUST
> The best reason to create a trust is to ensure that your assets can be transferred to your nominated beneficiaries in the way you want. For example, if you are reasonably wealthy and have young children, you would most likely not want them to inherit your wealth at a very young age if you die.
>
> If you create a trust in your will, the trust will take ownership of your assets until your children are of the right age to inherit. Trusts are quite flexible, so you can ensure that your children (or their guardians) receive an income while the children are still underage so that they can be properly cared for.
>
> Another good reason to have a trust is if you have a large estate and wish your assets to benefit a few generations of your family. So if you are 60 years old and have a 28-year-old child and a two-year-old grandchild, you might want to provide for your grandchild's education. A trust (especially one that is domiciled overseas) could be an ideal way to ensure that your wishes are met. There are some other situations too in which it is sensible to set up a trust. As with your will, make sure that you get proper advice and that your trust is correctly structured to meet your wishes.

Wills and the need for multiple wills

Every single adult should have a will – a legal document that states how you wish your possessions to be distributed when you die. I cannot think of one exception to this rule; whether you are a young person who is just starting your career or an elderly retiree, if you die without a will, you are creating massive problems for those you leave behind.

When you die, everything you own effectively becomes part of your estate. This is a legal requirement, and your estate must be closed down (wound up) according to a fixed procedure. There is a large body of law that relates to wills and estates, so it is worth ensuring that you have a legally valid will. If you have investments in various countries around the world, it is very important to find out what will happen to your assets in the event of your death. Do you need a will in that country? Who should draft a will for you? Will you need a legal representative to assist with finalising the process of transferring your assets to your beneficiaries?

I recommend that you approach a specialist to draft your will for you. In most instances these specialists are either lawyers or tax experts.

As a general guideline, you should review your will every year, or when there is a major change in your life – for instance, when there is a death in the family, if you get married or have a child, or if you get divorced or decide to separate from your partner.

World market indices

There are two main versions of the index that tracks shares across the globe. The developed market index is called the MSCI World Index, while the index representing developed markets plus emerging markets is called the MSCI All Country World Index (ACWI). This index consists of more than 3 000 companies listed on 50 stock exchanges around the world.

CHAPTER 12

MONEY AND RELATIONSHIPS

Regardless of whether you are in a long-term relationship or single, this chapter is essential reading, as the principles apply not only to partnerships but to your other relationships too.

If you are in a long-term relationship, whether married or not, money issues are bound to arise at some point. These issues are, without doubt, one of the leading causes of relationship troubles. Money can cause huge strain in a relationship. Likewise, a strong relationship can be very beneficial to your wealth.

If you are single, I like to recommend getting a 'savings buddy'. A savings buddy can hold you to account, just like a training partner at the gym or a running partner can. Good savings buddies can apply some positive mutual peer pressure to keep each other on track regarding savings goals.

In 2005 Jay Zagorsky, a psychologist, published a very comprehensive study on the economics of marriage, titled 'Marriage and Divorce's Impact on Wealth'. He found that the wealth of married people increased by around 14% for each year they were married. They generated nearly double the wealth of single people! According to Zagorsky, people who got divorced faced a 77% reduction in wealth. Deciding to get married can be the difference between financial freedom and financial destruction if you get it wrong. In other words, relationships and money are tightly intertwined.

If you are married or living with a partner, it is important to understand how each of you manages money. You need to discuss your money-management styles and not merely make assumptions based on your own personal philosophies, as it is rare for both parties in a relationship to have a similar attitude towards money. When you combine two different attitudes to money management, as most of us do in our relationships, it makes for some interesting discussions. In most instances, one person is more careful about spending, while the other person is more carefree with money. This is usually fertile ground for conflict – conflict that can be avoided through proper communication and planning.

Your personal relationship with money

The way you grew up has an enormous impact on your relationship with money, and that mindset is unlikely to change over your lifetime. But this 'hard-wired' relationship with money can be managed, provided you are honest about your money issues.

Those who grew up in a poor home will view money very differently from those who were raised in a wealthy home. However, this doesn't mean that all wealthy people will have the same attitude towards money. In fact, children from the same family often have completely different spending and saving behaviours.

When I meet a couple for the first time, I often find that one partner is largely uninvolved with the finances, while the other feels burdened by money decisions. When we start discussing attitudes towards money, there is frequently an underlying tension in the relationship because of this. I am regularly surprised by the dysfunctional ways in which couples deal with money. Here are some examples:

- One partner feels that the other spends too much money, so to avoid conflict the 'spender' hides his or her spending.
- A lawyer makes his wife pay for daily expenses with her own income, while he 'takes care' of the savings but doesn't share information with her about these 'savings'.
- A chartered accountant leaves all the investment decisions to her unemployed husband to bolster his confidence.
- A successful career woman earns far more than her husband but is afraid to tell him this for fear of undermining his self-worth.

- A high-powered executive constantly changes jobs because she gets bored or hates her boss and resigns, which places financial stress on the family when she is out of a job.
- An entrepreneur starts a new business and takes a mortgage against the family home as funding for the new business without telling his partner.
- One partner is blissfully ignorant of the family finances and investments because the other partner deals with all of them – until the partner who manages the finances commits suicide because the couple have serious financial problems.

I know psychologists would have a field day analysing these dynamics, but that is not my area of expertise. My focus is on helping people find ways to manage their money more effectively. This chapter offers some pointers you might find useful if you find yourself having money issues in your relationships.

Develop a plan for yourselves as a team

In my view, the traditional roles men and women often take on when managing money are totally flawed. In the past, men would control the money, while women controlled the household. There are so many problems with this that I am not even going to list them. However, I want to point out that women are very often better at budgeting and controlling money than men.

In my house, my wife is responsible for the budgeting, and I manage the investments. We are both well informed about what is happening with all aspects of our money. I have a good idea of how our budget is structured, while my wife knows how and where our money is invested. We have also agreed on a long-term investment strategy that meets both our needs. If I die before my wife, she is unlikely to change our investment strategy because she agrees with what we are doing.

This works well in our family because I tend to be more impulsive with spending. My wife is also very analytical and is known to our friends as the 'spreadsheet queen'. In other families, these roles might be reversed, but it is vital that each partner is well informed about the overall plan and that both are comfortable with what is happening.

I have met many widows (women tend to outlive men) who, throughout their married lives, left all the financial decisions to their husbands. When the husband passes away, the death is especially traumatic because the wife is suddenly confronted with a range of financial decisions that she is not prepared for.

I recall meeting a wonderful woman soon after she turned 70, whose husband had passed away a few months earlier. She was in a mess. She had been a senior politician and was a highly capable person but had not worried about finances for 40 years. She did not know how to do online banking, nor did she have any inkling of where and how her money was invested. It took us eight months to get a full understanding of where her money was invested, and another 12 months to get her up to speed on managing her finances.

When troubles in a relationship are caused by money, at least one partner feels disempowered in relation to money. This underlying anxiety needs to be addressed if you wish to keep the problems from snowballing. I find that couples can manage this by developing a long-term plan.

Long-term goals

I advise couples to start with their end goal in mind and then to work backwards from there. For example, if you and your partner are in your late 40s, you will need to agree on when you would like to be financially independent, where you would like to live at that time and what kind of lifestyle you want when you are no longer working. Once you have defined these long-term goals, you can calculate how much money you will need to fund them. This will determine how much you should save, what you can spend on luxuries and how you should invest your savings.

Once you have agreed on your main goals, each of you might take responsibility for certain aspects of your finances. On a regular basis (quarterly, six-monthly or yearly), you should review your plans and how you have progressed towards your goals. It is important that you are both part of the process and share a common purpose so that you can hold each other accountable to reach your shared goals. This helps the more anxious person because there is a plan in place, while the more relaxed person might realise that there is some work to be done.

Investment decisions for couples

I think it is a little easier for couples with different money attitudes to work together on a budget than it is to manage their investments together. First, each partner will have a different level of financial literacy. If one partner is not familiar with investments, it will be difficult for that person to understand and feel comfortable with investment decisions.

Second, individual people have a specific level of risk tolerance when it comes to investments. Some will be comfortable with investing in a higher-risk investment, and when it loses money for a time, they will maintain their composure. Others simply cannot tolerate any kind of loss on an investment for any period. In this situation, couples need to figure out how to manage their investments so that both parties can sleep at night.

It is important to understand that your tolerance for investment risk is a hard-wired psychological trait that is unrelated to other traits. You might be a natural risk taker when it comes to fast cars, skydiving and other physical activities, but you might be totally risk averse with investments.

Generally, issues around risk only become problematic when one of the partners has an extreme attitude to risk – either too risk prone or too risk averse. To an extent, you can achieve some balance in your attitude to investment risk by increasing your knowledge about investing.

I am not suggesting that both partners need to study investments. When I meet people who are in a relationship, I always try to meet them together. I usually insist that they are both part of the planning process when we determine how their capital will be invested and what sort of risk must be taken. If one partner is my main contact, it is still vital that the other partner knows what we are doing, how the money is being invested and what could happen if the stock market crashes. This is important because, as a financial planner, I do not want to meet the other partner for the first time when my main contact has passed away. The whole point of financial planning is to ensure continuity and that the financial impact of loss on the couple or the family is limited.

Planning for the worst: When your partner dies

Fewer couples are getting married, but they are still buying houses and creating investments together. In these situations, it is important to plan and document what will happen if one partner dies. I have seen a few too many situations where a couple buys a home together and one partner dies in an accident. Often the remaining partner is forced to sell the home because there was only one source of income, and the remaining partner can no longer repay the bond. I have also experienced cases in which the family of the deceased are not familiar with the financial situation of the couple and a dispute arises around money. So it should be very clear that an up-to-date will is necessary, but considering the financial implications of an unexpected death is important too. You might need to take life assurance on each other's lives in addition to creating a will.

It is a fact that people in a long-term relationship tend to live longer and happier lives than their single counterparts. The stability that a relationship provides to both individuals is clearly important. Money is a crucial aspect of life, so it is vital to ensure that couples manage their money in partnership so it can become a foundation of their relationship and not a problem area.

Planning for the next generation: What to teach your children about money

Some families are quite open with their children about the family's finances. Everyone in the family has an idea of how much income is generated within the family, how much is spent, and what the joint financial goals of the family are. Everyone has a vote on how much is spent on holidays, and the family decides together what necessary trade-offs must be made if money is tight.

In other families, money is a subject that is not discussed. But if you have children, it is vital to teach them about it. I firmly believe that teaching the next generation about money and educating them on how to budget, save and invest should also be part of the school curriculum. However, parents must take primary responsibility for this important life skill.

When children are old enough, they should be given the opportunity to give some input on how money will be spent on schooling or tertiary education and how this should be weighed against the need for new tech gadgets, or spending on clothes and entertainment. Learning how to prioritise spending and how to delay gratification is a skill that is best mastered when you are young!

I came across an extreme example of teaching kids at a young age in a relatively wealthy man who gave each of his children a sizeable lump sum when they turned 13. Each child at the time received the equivalent of $85 000! This amount was paid into an investment account that the child could monitor online. Only the parents could authorise withdrawals from the account – a vital safety net for this exercise! The parents explained to the child that the money in the account should be sufficient to pay for the remaining five years of school, as well as cover allowances for entertainment, clothes and tech devices, such as laptops and phones. To start off, each child learnt about how they could invest their money so that it would grow over the five years, while also offering the flexibility to pay out expenses at different times of the year. If the child managed to finish school with money remaining, the child could use the money for anything. Of the three children in this family, the father told me that two did very well. They budgeted carefully and invested in balanced mutual funds. Both were left with sizeable amounts after finishing school. However, one child was not so successful: 'My youngest daughter,' explained the man, 'is a caring and kind soul who just wanted to give her money to the needy.'

Money and emotions are inextricably interlinked. If you are in a serious relationship, it is vital to ensure that both of you are able to discuss issues around money and how they will affect the relationship. I am a big fan of author and public speaker Brené Brown. Her talks on YouTube and her book *Daring Greatly* have been invaluable to me and many of my clients.

CHAPTER 13

INVESTMENT INSIGHTS FROM THE RICH AND FAMOUS

Throughout this book I have tried to show you that financial freedom is possible for anybody. I have provided suggestions and scenarios that can be adopted by anyone at any level of wealth and financial literacy. Much of my personal learning has come from dealing with financially successful people, lots of reading and research, and the teachings of investing masters like Charlie Munger and Warren Buffett. I believe we can all learn from people who have achieved incredible investment success without having to emulate their strategies. The more we can learn from these greats, the more chance we have of reaching our own version of greatness.

    I have been redefining the concept of financial success for myself as I have grown older. Initially, I simply wanted to be wealthy – with homes on every continent and a private jet parked on the runway waiting for me. By the time I reached my 30s, I had completely different priorities: philanthropy had become a driving force in my life, and I really wanted to achieve financial freedom for my wife, who is naturally anxious about personal finances. Now that I am in my 40s, we have achieved a measure of financial freedom: we don't have to work any more. We could sell our home, our businesses and retire to a small house in the country. However, my goals have shifted once again. I want to secure our financial position so that my wife can live in any country in the world without having to reduce her standard of living. At the same time, I feel an increasing drive to escalate our philanthropic efforts further. There is so much need in the world and I have the energy and ability to help more people. The need for a private jet has passed, although I admit the Covid-19 pandemic did reignite the debate with my wife for a few days.

I am not sure how to define greatness or success for you, because I think it will be different for everybody. As an example, anyone with limited financial means and an unremarkable career could be a great parent. Similarly, a Wall Street titan might have incredible wealth but be counting the cost of this wealth in broken family relationships and a lack of close friends. It is certainly not my purpose to define success for you. That is your job! However, I would like to share with you some experiences and lessons that I have accumulated in my more than 20 years of advising, managing and working with successful, wealthy people.

Successful people don't tell you how hard they work

> *'If you ask a skinny woman what her diet is, she'll probably tell you she doesn't really have a diet – works out a bit, and eats whatever she wants, but makes some effort to avoid junk food. Ask entrepreneurs how they became so successful, and they'll say they simply had an idea, started a business, and it took off somehow. And they'll all be lying. People would rather hear that success comes from luck than from hard work. The next time you hear a successful person say that they didn't have to work very hard for their success, don't believe them. They're lying – not because they're jerks, but because other people are jerks and will punish them for being honest.'*
>
> **– John Fawkes, fitness expert**

It is no coincidence that the best sportspeople, musicians, academics, business leaders and investors work very hard at their chosen careers. Importantly, they work hard consistently over long periods to ensure that they know more, have better skills and are more prepared than everybody else.

What is rarely mentioned is that being successful is often about sticking to your task when everyone else is relaxing and enjoying themselves.

I had to remind myself of this regularly while writing this book, because I was also running my business, working on my fitness goals, trying to be a good husband and friend, and keeping up my media work! So the only time I could allocate to writing this book was on weekends, public holidays and early weekday mornings – usually starting from 4:30 a.m. One positive result of this experience was that I gave up watching TV because it was not adding to my life and certainly was not making me a better husband.

Surround yourself with successful people

'You're the average of the five people you spend most of your time with.'
– **Jim Rohn, US entrepreneur**

This is one of the most profound insights I want to share with you. It is no accident that one person acting completely alone rarely achieves greatness in any endeavour. The people around you really do matter, and you need to ensure that you are spending time with the right people.

If you are a parent, this is one of the factors to consider when selecting schools, sports clubs and leisure pursuits for your children: always try to help them spend time with people who embody the attributes that you want to see in them.

Similarly, if you aspire to greatness in your career, spend time with the people who are on the path you are aiming for. If you work in a low-performance business or one that has values that clash with your own, you need to make a change. We spend most of our time at work, and a bad work environment will have a negative impact on our whole life.

I strongly advise entrepreneurs to spend a few hours every month with other successful entrepreneurs. It is very difficult for a business leader to interact with other leaders in a meaningful and constructive way. This means you need to make a conscious effort to engage with other entrepreneurs you admire so that you learn from them and open yourself up to being positively influenced by them, especially when you are going through a bad patch.

If you are in a slump and cannot find a way to kick-start yourself, look at the people around you. Reid Hoffman, founder of LinkedIn, said, 'The fastest way to change yourself is to hang out with people who are already the way you want to be.' It is very possible that the people with whom you are spending the most time are part of the reason you cannot recover from your slump, and unless you start spending time with different people, you are probably going to remain bogged down.

If it is not possible to spend time with successful people, you can certainly spend less time with negative or destructive people. The next best thing to spending time with successful people is to allocate more time to reading about successful people, especially reading their books and articles.

I make it a part of my routine to read biographies of successful people from a variety of different fields. This includes army generals, business leaders, entrepreneurs, sportspeople (especially great coaches) and respected religious leaders. I may never get to meet Bill Gates, Michael Jordan or Warren Buffett, but I can read what they have written or what has been written about them and try to learn more about them from other authors.

If you want change, start with your state of mind

Fifteen years ago, my wife and I found ourselves becoming more depressed about the state of the world. It felt as though politicians were destroying all that was good, including the planet. I happened to read an interview with a renowned business leader who remarked that he had stopped watching and reading the news every day because it was always filled with negativity. He claimed that his life had changed significantly for the better.

So my wife and I stopped watching the daily news and weekly actuality programmes. Owing to the nature of our careers, however, we continued to read one daily business newspaper and monthly business magazines. From that time onwards, our lives improved noticeably. We are generally much more upbeat and positive about our world than ever before. We try to resolve the problems we can control, we tolerate the problems we cannot control, and we plan around the problems we can avoid.

If you have a money-spending problem, try not to spend time with people who have the same problem, because they will make it seem acceptable for you to give up on your saving ambitions. If everyone around you makes excuses for their shortcomings rather than looking for ways to succeed, it is natural for this to affect you. Rather spend time with people who are saving money and who appreciate the value of investments. Those are the role models you should be emulating instead of people who look glamorous, drive expensive cars and live in big houses. Their lifestyle is very probably funded by excessive debt.

Patience: The difference between a great investment and a disaster

If there is one differentiator between wealthy people and those who are not, it is probably patience. Lack of patience is the reason for most of the worst investment decisions. For instance, investors might buy very risky investments in the hope that they will increase in value quickly, only to see those investments blow up. Or investors run out of patience with a great investment that they believe is not increasing in value fast enough, and so they sell it too early, usually mere weeks or months before its value starts rising like a hot-air balloon.

Really great investments tend to gradually drift up in price over time. They often go through periods where nothing seems to happen, but when you review them after a few months, you notice how much they have grown. I tend to be wary of investments that rise too rapidly; gravity applies in the world of investments as much as it does in physics.

Here is what Paul Samuelson, the first American winner of the Nobel Prize for Economics and economic advisor to two US presidents, had to say: 'Investing should be more like watching paint dry or watching grass grow. If you want excitement, take $800 and go to Las Vegas.'

Know what you are buying

If you have a 'friend' in the money business who is always telling you about some new product or fund that is certain to make money quickly, it is time to find a new friend. Many intelligent and financially sophisticated people get caught in investment scams because they trust their friends rather than their own judgement. As Peter Lynch, a famous US mutual fund manager and author, aptly said: 'Know what you own, and know why you own it.'

This is the primary reason I do not invest significant portions of money in hedge funds, cryptocurrencies or structured products. They tend to be very complex and use sophisticated algorithms and legal structures that seem amazing and without any real flaws. But as I am neither a mathematical genius nor do I understand complex derivatives or financial structures, how can I be sure that I know what I own? The short answer is that I can't, so I rather avoid buying them.

I also remain sceptical about hedge fund managers who accumulate billions in personal wealth in a few short years by managing other people's wealth. Whereas Warren Buffett accumulated his wealth over 40 years, some hedge fund managers accumulate billions in three to five years, and I cannot shake the suspicion that they did this by overcharging their clients or through financial trickery that might catch up with them in later years.

Average can be exceptional

In the world of investments, there are many ways to make money. If you are like me and prefer investing in shares or mutual funds, it is worth considering index-tracking investments, which are quite simple and low-cost. For example, you can buy one mutual fund that aims to replicate the performance of the largest 500 shares in the US stock market. The S&P 500 allows you to buy an index-tracking investment that simply buys the shares in this index in the most cost-effective way possible. It might seem boring and could potentially limit your growth, but consider what John C. Bogle, the father of index investing in the USA and founder of Vanguard, said: 'Don't look for the needle in the haystack. Just buy the haystack!' You might think he was biased, but history has proved that only a small number of mutual funds will beat the index over longer periods.

Even the greatest share investor of all time believes in index investing for his loved ones. In his will, this is what Warren Buffett has instructed his lawyers to do once he has passed away: 'My advice to the trustee could not be more simple: put 10% of the cash in short-term government bonds and 90% in a very low-cost S&P 500 index fund. I believe the trust's long-term results from this policy will be superior to those attained by most investors.'

Investing is not about being active or entertained

> *'If investing is entertaining, if you're having fun, you're probably not making any money. Good investing is boring.'*
> **– George Soros, hedge fund manager and philanthropist**

'The individual investor should act consistently as an investor and not as a speculator.' These are the words of Ben Graham, original mentor to Warren Buffett and firm advocate of value investing long before it became a global asset-management trend.

When stock markets or currencies take a major fall, investors feel a nearly irresistible urge to *do something*. But in times of major uncertainty in the investment world, especially when everything is going down, it is often best to do nothing. I realise that is like asking you to run into a building when it is on fire and everyone else is running away, but in the investment arena this is often your best course of action. While the urge to act is hard-wired in our brains and was a really helpful impulse when we lived among wild animals, these types of impulsive urges are nearly always fatal to wealth creation.

In truth, no one knows what will happen tomorrow, and therefore we should really think carefully and make considered investment decisions. So my advice is rather to focus on buying quality assets you believe will gradually appreciate in value over a long period and then try to forget about them.

'We ignore outlooks and forecasts ... we're lousy at it and we admit it ... everyone else is lousy too, but most people won't admit it,' says Martin J. Whitman, fund manager and academic.

If you want your investments to be like an action movie or high-intensity sport, you are probably going to make some real losses over your lifetime.

Be prepared for investment crashes

Rising markets, especially those that have been rising for a long time, are more dangerous to your financial health than falling markets. This might seem contradictory, because a rising market means your existing investments will be appreciating in value, so your overall financial position is improving. Unfortunately, this also means that you will be paying more for assets if you invest new money in a rising market.

Many fortunes have been lost by investing lump sums in a rising market, because people tend to invest the largest amount of money in the months before a major market crash. Unfortunately, no one can predict when a market will crash, nor can they predict when the recovery will start after the crash.

I believe it is impossible to be a successful long-term investor if you build your strategy on market timing. This applies to all major markets, including shares and property. Rather ensure that you are constantly invested and are prepared for a major market crash. As John C. Bogle says, 'If you have trouble imagining a 20% loss in the stock market, you shouldn't be in stocks.' This means it is best to buy only assets you are prepared to hold through a market crash. If you buy a property, you should be comfortable holding that property even if there is another financial crisis that causes the price to drop by 20% or more. If you have new capital to invest and your chosen investment market is rising, try to feed your money into that market over a period of months. By contrast, if you are unlucky enough to invest in the months before a crash, you might find that your average price is not so high that you never recover your capital.

If you are a property investor, it might not be possible to buy your investments over the period of a few months. In this case, ensure that your purchase price is reasonable and that you exercise real patience and restraint when buying. Rather miss out on a good deal than end up buying an overpriced property that costs you money.

J. Paul Getty, an American industrialist rated the richest person in the world when he was alive, once said: 'Buy when everyone else is selling and hold until everyone else is buying. That's not just a catchy slogan. It's the very essence of successful investing.'

Investing in rising vs. falling markets

As an investment advisor to wealthy private individuals, I have always found it more difficult to keep my clients rational in a market that has been climbing strongly for an extended period. I find that investor expectations can become unrealistic in rising markets because they start to believe that markets will climb forever and that there is no risk of investment losses. In more than 20 years as an investment advisor, I have only been fired by a handful of clients, and all of them did so in a rising market when I was advising greater caution.

My best example is a highly educated and financially literate young couple who had saved aggressively and had the clear objective of becoming financially independent before the age of 50. They were well on their way to this goal and had by then been clients for about six years. The local and global economies were really struggling, interest rates were low, and unemployment was high and rising. As often happens in these conditions, the stock market was rising despite all the bad news. My clients were keen to invest some large lump sums into the stock market and I was advising them to exercise restraint by rather investing their money in batches over a 12-month period. They took the advice, and, after the first three months, the markets continued to rise very strongly. This upset my clients and we had a heated meeting, during which they fired me for being too cautious. We had reached the end of our relationship. Unfortunately, they had been dazzled by the returns promised by a hedge fund manager who had a high-risk strategy. They moved all their assets to this manager. Three months later the markets tumbled, causing them to lose 30% of their assets. Had they remained cautious in their strategy and continued to feed their money into the market in batches, their losses would have been minimal.

Borrowing money for investment

Good investment advisors will tell you that it is usually a bad idea to borrow money to invest in the stock market. This is particularly true if you need the market to rise so that you can afford your debt repayments. Similarly, borrowing money for a property investment often leads to financial ruin. As well-known author and investor Robert Kiyosaki cautions, 'Remember, debt is not to be used lightly. It demands great respect and education.'

I advise clients to treat debt incurred to buy investments in much the same way as a construction engineer treats explosives: if you do not know what you are doing, rather stay far away.

Of course, explosives can be very helpful in the right hands and in the right situation, and for large-scale projects. If you take the time to educate yourself properly and use debt in a very controlled way, it can help you build a profitable investment portfolio more efficiently. As a start, ensure that you are able to easily afford your monthly debt repayments. If your monthly debt repayments total $1 000 a month, ensure that you can afford to repay $2 000 per month.

Always plan for the unexpected too – for example, if you lose your job, your property tenant absconds and doesn't pay rent, or the company you are investing in forgoes dividend repayments for a few quarters. You need to have ready access to liquid capital, such as funds in a money market account that you can use if for some reason you cannot afford your debt repayments for a few months. This will ensure that you are not beholden to the bank that originally lent you the money.

If you are struggling to make a debt repayment on an asset and you need to rely on a bank to assist you, your life will be very difficult. First, banks no longer understand the concept of risk management; they tend to avoid risk at all costs. If you are unable to repay your debt for a short period, your bank will force you to sell assets to pay down your debt. In this situation, the bank is only interested in recovering the value of your debt. I have seen how a bank can ruin property investors because it auctions off these properties at ridiculously low prices to ensure that it recovers the value of the debt. So investors are left with very little, while a little bit more patience on the part of the bank would have helped both parties tremendously.

If you know that you have done your homework and you understand your chosen investment market properly, you should still be very selective when buying your investment with debt. Wait for times when your chosen market offers excellent buying opportunities. If you wish to invest in shares, wait until the stock market has fallen significantly – by more than 20%. If you wish to invest in property, remember that a situation like the financial crisis of 2008/09 was a brilliant buying opportunity: many investors had bought properties they could not afford and when the banks came under pressure, the prices of properties around the world crashed. This presented some great opportunities to buy if you were prepared to be patient and wait for prices to recover over the next few years. Finally, try to ensure that you understand the current interest rate environment when you borrow to invest.

After 2008, central banks around the world dropped interest rates dramatically to kick-start their countries' economies. This meant borrowing costs were falling for investors who were borrowing money to invest, which is ideal for the investors. Conversely, when interest rates are very low, be prepared for them to rise significantly over some years. Rising interest rates are not good news for investors because they cause prices to fall. Property and share prices usually fall when interest rates rise, especially if they rise quickly or unexpectedly. If you are borrowing to invest and are unprepared for increased monthly repayments while your investment is decreasing in value, this could really hurt you.

One of the ways to limit or manage your risks when borrowing money to invest is to buy income-generating assets. Generating investment income while you are paying off the debt means that you can repay your debt more quickly. This will improve your monthly cash flow, especially in the early stages of your investment career.

Don't sacrifice your ethics in the pursuit of money

It might seem strange to talk about ethics and investing as part of the same topic, but long-term financial success is often linked to a sound moral and ethical foundation. You need to know why you are spending time and effort on your finances and, more importantly, know and ensure that you have a very strong moral compass to guide you when things get tough.

A powerful personal vision that motivates you combined with a strong set of personal values will be essential for long-term success. People who have a weak moral compass tend to make bad decisions over the long term and usually find themselves in financial trouble because they were willing to take short cuts for rapid financial gain.

Famous US investor and author Philip Fisher said: 'The stock market is filled with individuals who know the price of everything, but the value of nothing.' It is usually quite easy to recover from a financial setback that was made in good faith, but it is nearly impossible to recover from an ethical lapse. Very often the financial impact of unethical behaviour is devastating and will limit your recovery potential forever. Rather stay true to your values, remain ethical, focus on long-term gain, and worry less about the short term – no one else knows what will happen in the future either!

CHAPTER 14

FINANCIAL BLUNDERS TO AVOID

After more than two decades of dealing with investors and their money, I have accumulated a sizeable collection of horror stories of how bad financial decisions have harmed, and even destroyed, people's lives. Most of these mistakes can be grouped into a few basic categories. While the categories I present here are not all-inclusive, they show the most common mistakes I have encountered. There is something to be learnt from each one.

Overspending and excessive debt

Without doubt, most people who are in constant financial difficulty are those who always spend more than they earn. Sadly, these same people seem to repeat this behaviour over their entire lifetime, without learning from past mistakes.

I find it terribly frustrating to observe this kind of behaviour, because the solution to the problem seems so simple. I often compare overspending to similarly self-sabotaging behaviour – like overeating, not sleeping enough, or not exercising. Any outsider can see the problem, but the person who is in trouble cannot stop. Access to money is a vital part of our lives and our wellbeing. I am no expert on the human brain, but I do know that money and psychology are intertwined. Many people find it hard to separate their sense of self-worth from their financial wellbeing.

One of my long-standing clients lost her husband to cancer a few years ago. She had faithfully nursed him through his last days and they had carefully planned their finances so that she would be financially secure once he had passed on. But they could not have planned for the depression she suffered after he died – a depression that was nearly her undoing, as it caused radical overspending: she started spending money on seemingly innocuous items that did not cause alarm until her spending was tallied up over a few months. As I looked through her credit card slips, I realised that she had been visiting a convenience store 20 to 30 times a day. Each time she would buy a magazine, a pack of chewing gum, or some other similarly low-priced item. To outsiders, she seemed to be coping well with the loss of her husband. But when I tallied the amounts, I realised that she was fast eroding her precious investment capital and would be destitute within a few years. Fortunately, she managed to overcome the problem with support from her adult children, through counselling, and with some careful financial coaching.

A common problem is overspending through excessive debt, which is often the case with vehicle purchases. Motor manufacturers are brilliant marketing businesses that specialise in selling expensive vehicles people do not need. This problem is exacerbated by enthralling TV shows like *Top Gear* and *The Grand Tour*. To make matters worse, banks and other financial institutions have been party to this racket for decades: they find creative ways for people with limited financial means to buy expensive cars and then pay them off over extended periods. Between the banks and the motor manufacturers, many people have been conned into calculating the affordability of vehicles by the amount they need to repay every month rather than the total capital value they will spend on them over many years.

Even some of the most financially literate people fall into the vehicle-overspending trap. I know some chartered accountants who would overspend on their vehicle purchases every three years. They simply 'had to' own a large SUV because they needed the extra space on the rare occasion when their children's friends needed to be transported to soccer!

Modern vehicles are very well made. So it is possible to buy a high-quality, safe used car at a much lower price than a new one. If your goal is financial freedom, avoid expensive cars, as this is a great way to save. I am convinced that if everyone spent less on cars, there would be many more home owners with paid-off home loans.

Underspending

To younger people who have grown up in financially stable homes or in times of economic prosperity, underspending is an unthinkable problem. But I have many elderly clients who grew up in difficult times, when the world was in a severe economic depression. They often went hungry as children, and many could not afford to go to school. As a result, they grew up preparing for the next disaster. They saved every cent 'for a rainy day', and when they retired as wealthy people, they could not change the habits of a lifetime.

When my wife's grandmother died in her 90s, the family found many unused towels, clothes, cosmetics and other gifts that she had been given during her lifetime. She had not been able to bring herself to throw away anything until it had fallen apart. She did not want to use the new towels and linen herself, as she thought this was wasteful. She did not die a pauper, but she lived a very compromised lifestyle because of her fear of running out of money.

I realise this might not seem such a big issue, but many people live very depressed lives because they are so afraid of running out of money. They avoid spending on medical care or proper housing, and often live an isolated and unhappy existence.

When I advise people who have a similar problem with underspending, I try to encourage them to budget for a single 'luxury' expense every year. Most often, they end up taking their children or grandchildren on holiday as a luxury expense. I think this is a great compromise as everyone benefits from the experience.

It will be interesting to see what the long-term impacts of the Covid-19 pandemic are: Will they cause a new generation of people to live in fear of a major economic crash? It is my hope that a new generation of savers will be created who can balance their lives and finances more successfully than previous generations.

Short-term thinking

I often receive messages from people who have just started out in their careers and are investing their first savings. The most common question they ask me is this: 'By when will my investment generate enough growth so that I can retire early?' I reply honestly and tell them that it could take them seven to ten years to make their first million. Most never contact me again.

Investing in productive assets (those that should grow in value by more than the inflation rate) is not an exact science. You could make a sound investment in a great asset and be derailed because of a random event like a terrorist attack in another country. But such an event should not prompt you to sell all your investments immediately. On the contrary, you should probably buy more of the same investment, if possible, and wait for its recovery. Recovery might take a few months or years. Unfortunately, the patience required to wait for this recovery is beyond many – especially inexperienced investors. Investing money is simple in concept but sometimes awfully difficult in practice. It takes a bit of common sense, some intelligence, but most importantly it takes a whole lot of patience and determination!

Overconfidence in an investment

John A. came to my offices three years after selling his tech business for more than $10 million. His story was not unusual: he was a successful, intelligent businessman who thought that he would easily manage his own investments. Because he was so smart and successful, he believed he could use his intelligence and business skills to conquer the investment markets. However, his overconfidence in his investment abilities and his need for control were nearly his undoing. After three years of managing his own money, he had lost nearly $3 million. It took John and me two years to develop a good understanding, because he struggled to relinquish control of his investments. But eventually he decided that it was easier for him to run a business than it was for him to manage his money.

John started another business and used a portion of his capital on that venture. This gave him something constructive to do with his energy and a part of his cash. We reached a small compromise where John invested a small portion of his money in investments that I tend to avoid. He then gave me free rein to manage the balance of his investments. Thankfully, some of John's picks worked well (especially his early start into cryptocurrencies), while I generated more predictable growth with a more diversified portfolio of assets. I am happy to report that investor and advisor are both content with this arrangement!

Medical specialists (surgeons in particular), lawyers and tech millionaires often believe that their past success in a different field qualifies them for automatic financial expertise. This self-belief is especially prevalent if they are mathematically gifted, because they believe markets can be reduced to formulas. But a track record of success in a job that has led to real wealth creation in a certain field doesn't automatically make someone a successful investor. The markets have humbled many intelligent people over hundreds of years, especially those who are overconfident or arrogant.

To be successful with investments, you need to be confident in your abilities, but humble enough to know that you will regularly make mistakes. Arrogance and overconfidence might lead to financial success over a few months or years, but eventually the markets will humble even the most successful investors. History's greatest investors often talk more about their (many) mistakes than their successes. In fact, many of them will acknowledge that they worked very hard over many years, but they were also lucky. This type of humility is a key ingredient in long-term investment success.

The difference between Warren Buffett and similarly intelligent investors from his era, for example, is that he never got caught up in his success. He always reminds people that he was lucky enough to be born at the right time, in the right country, with parents who could afford to pay for his education. This humility means that even when he has strong convictions about an investment idea, he fully anticipates that he could be wrong and makes plans to ensure that he will survive if he makes a big error.

For overconfident investors who believe that they can outwit the market and are more intelligent than their peers, early successes can be lethal. It leads them to make highly risky investment decisions that tend to destroy their entire wealth when they make a mistake. The late Sir John Templeton – a pioneer in both financial investment and philanthropy – maintained that he was correct with 51% of his investment decisions over his lifetime. Considering his astounding success over decades, we should all be prepared to be wrong with one out of two investment decisions.

Fear or greed

Undoubtedly, the biggest speculative bubble of the decade from 2011 to 2020 was Bitcoin, or the cryptocurrency market in general. I am not arguing that cryptocurrencies are useless or that they are a scam. Truthfully, I do not know how they will eventually affect the world of money. There have been many examples of great ideas or technologies that have not achieved wide acceptance. Cryptocurrencies might change the world, or they might fade away to be replaced by something else – we cannot accurately predict the outcome.

However, I can tell you that many unscrupulous sharks are operating in the world of cryptocurrencies and that they are using tried and tested techniques to catch unsuspecting people who are motivated by greed or FOMO – fear of missing out. In the beginning, cryptos were only followed by a few hardcore tech-savvy believers who wanted to find a way to change the economic and political systems of the world. The most notable example was Bitcoin and, while it started slowly, investors increasingly became aware of it, and eventually it became a topic of conversation everywhere. People across the board – from hairdressers to academics, from doctors to mechanics – started speculating in Bitcoin. Unfortunately, many people borrowed money, cashed in their savings, or accessed their retirement funds to put money into Bitcoin. The rate of growth of the price of Bitcoin was astonishing, and ordinary people became instant US dollar millionaires – until the bubble burst. At its peak, in December 2017, Bitcoin was priced at more than $19 000 per coin. On Christmas Day, just over a year later, the price plummeted to $3 777, a drop of more than 80%. I am concerned by the many people who sold their homes, cashed in their retirement funds and put all their savings into Bitcoin at $19 000. Bitcoin has since regained some of its losses, but many investors had cashed out already as they could not tolerate any further loss. It is tempting to judge people who cashed out harshly, and we might argue that they should have been more patient. However, the truth is that they actually could not afford the initial risks and should never have been speculating in volatile assets in the first place.

The network-marketing sharks who were promoting cryptos as a way of taking control of your life so that you wouldn't need to work nine to five for a boss are, of course, now living lives of luxury. They hadn't invested their own money in cryptos but were selling courses on how to get rich! If a new speculative bubble starts to form in some other asset, these network-marketing sharks will move on to a new generation of people who are in desperate need of a financial miracle.

Since I started in the investment industry in the mid-1990s, I have seen more than 20 large investment scams collapse. At the most basic level, they are run by people who successfully manage to convince others to part with their capital because they are fearful or greedy. Unscrupulous operators are experts at playing to your emotions once they have identified the one that drives you. This has caused untold damage in many people's lives. In many cases, retirees were the main victims of these scams, and some of them committed suicide rather than face life without savings. Retirees who have insufficient funds start searching for one or two investments that might enable them to make up the additional capital they require. Because they are often desperate, they become easy targets for unscrupulous operators looking to make a quick buck.

Most scams are based on partially believable facts, and property is often used as a cornerstone of scams. For some reason, investors like to know that their money will be invested in property and that the specific property or properties they are buying are much better than anything else in the market. It is fear or greed that allows them to deceive themselves when they are sold a story.

Other scams that have worked in the past are sold as high-risk, high-return structured investments. The promoters of these scams claim that the exact nature of these investments must be kept secret so that other people do not find out about them. In addition, they limit access to the investments by making them exclusive, so that you must be 'invited' to invest. (Take the time to read about Bernie Madoff if you want an example of a massive scam that ran for decades and cost investors more than $60 billion.)

A third variety of scam that has been successful is sold as a pooled investment in a private business (or group of businesses) that is doing very well at the time. Investors are told that, in fact, these businesses are doing so well that they are expanding rapidly and need capital to meet their growth obligations. Often the businesses are described as manufacturing companies that have suddenly landed big orders from new clients and need money to buy more machinery or raw materials to fulfil the orders. The businesses are so sure of making a profit from these new orders that they are willing to pay high interest rates if you lend them money. These scams are risky or quite tenuous, even though there are businesses in this position that do have legitimate orders. However, I am always very sceptical if someone approaches me with this type of proposition. My default view is that anything that offers too high a return is a scam unless I can be absolutely convinced otherwise.

I maintain that nothing can take the place of careful, thorough research when it comes to making investment decisions. I advise my clients to read what the experts say, never to be afraid to ask 'stupid' questions, and to maintain scepticism in the face of get-rich-quick promises. When a financial commentator writes that they would not invest in something or that they cannot understand it, be wary! That person is trying to tell you to treat the investment as you would a swarm of angry bees – avoid! Always remember the old saying that if it sounds too good to be true, then it probably is.

Blind trust and family advice

In my work as a professional financial planner, I have stopped counting the number of times clients have told me to 'just go ahead, I trust you'. While this is a lovely compliment to any advisor, it is also scary.

All investors should have some knowledge of how their money is being invested. If you make use of the services of a financial planner or asset manager, make sure that you have a basic understanding of what your advisor is doing. You do not need to be an expert, nor do you need in-depth knowledge of what is happening, but you should make it your business to know all the basics of what is going on with your finances.

You should be particularly inquisitive if you are relying on family members or close friends to help you with your investments. Remember that it is not rude to ask questions about your own money. You should always ask how your advisor is getting paid and where their money is invested. A few years ago, one of my favourite clients called to tell me that his son-in-law was joining a private bank as a wealth manager. My client felt obliged to support his daughter and her husband. We parted ways amicably a few weeks later, with the reassurance from my side that he was welcome to return if he wanted to rejoin as a client.

After 12 months, he called me to admit that he had made a big mistake. He was simply not getting what he wanted from his son-in-law and felt let down. We agreed that he should persist for a few more months before making the decision to rejoin. Another 12 months passed, and he called on a Monday to tell me that he could no longer continue working with his son-in-law and had told the family so over the weekend. He had not lost any money, but he never felt able to have an open discussion with his son-in-law to discuss his money and especially his concerns. There are times when friends, family and money can be a powerful combination, but in many instances it is often a potent recipe for disaster.

Buying high and selling low

Without fail, certain investors will avoid the stock market when it is offering great value and will invest only when it is really expensive and due for a crash. Why does this happen?

The stock market offers great value when bad news dominates. Certain investors simply cannot disregard this news and, because of fear, will not invest their money. They will invest only when all the financial news is good and the stock markets have been booming for some years. Sadly, we know what will happen once they have invested their money: the market crashes and they sell out in a panic at a major loss. This pattern repeats itself every five to seven years, which is just long enough for people to forget the lessons of the past few years.

You can invest successfully only if you remain invested when the whole world seems to be falling apart. I am not saying that this is easy to do, but it is the only way to ensure long-term success.

Procrastination

We all know that nothing good was ever accomplished by procrastination – in fact, procrastinators tend to accomplish nothing at all! However, procrastination is particularly problematic when it relates to money management, because your problems literally compound themselves. If you delay paying off your debt or starting to invest your savings, the power of compounded growth will work against you, not for you.

Lack of balance

There can never be an absolute view on money, especially not regarding investments. If you want to be a successful saver and investor, you need to ensure that you budget for fun or luxury items too. Without some balance, you might be very disciplined for a limited time, but you will eventually crack under pressure, and possibly erode or destroy your quality of life.

When making investment decisions, try to ensure you keep a balanced view. For example, if you strongly believe that the stock market will crash, do not sell all your shares. Rather reduce your investment in shares, but keep some money invested in the event that you are wrong. Apply this basic approach to all your money decisions: always try to remain balanced and humble.

CONCLUSION

Investing can be simple, but I believe most people find it difficult because it requires patience, discipline and rational thinking in times of great stress and uncertainty. Unfortunately, human beings are not designed to be rational in stressful situations. If we feel threatened and fear we may come to harm, physical or financial, our brains demand that we fight or run away. These hard-wired responses are very difficult to resist.

If we give in to our primal urges when managing our investments, we are very likely to lose money. So if we are serious about achieving financial freedom, we need to find tools that will help us manage our emotions when everyone else is panicking. This might seem unnatural, but I strongly believe that all we need to do is simply reframe the way we look at the world.

In a big stock market crash, I always try to look for opportunities to buy great assets at a discount. My whole approach is that when everything is on sale, I would be foolish to ignore the opportunity to buy quality investments at ridiculously low prices. But I can only do this if my mental approach is right and my financial position is not compromised by a market crash. This means I need to have an emergency fund in place. I also need access to money at short notice. There is nothing complicated about starting an emergency fund – it just takes discipline. The difficult part is having the discipline to avoid wasting my money on worthless stuff that will give me momentary pleasure (like a new car) but will prevent me from allocating money to my investments. This is a behavioural habit anyone can develop if they have the motivation.

The inspiration for change and the motivation to stick to new habits must come from within. You need a vision for your life that will motivate you to stick to your good habits consistently, every day. This motivation could come from your desire to provide for your family, or it could be based on your desire to see the world, or to provide education opportunities to the needy. It does not really matter what your motivation is, but it must be powerful enough to keep you going when you want to give up. If you struggle with motivation, get a training buddy to help you stick to your financial goals. Positive peer pressure from people you respect can be an incredible force for good in your life, so use it to help you.

Financial goals can seem like large mountains that are impossible to climb. If you feel like you are trying to attain the impossible, stop looking at the summit! Then set yourself one small goal at a time and work towards it. When you reach this goal, set the next one, and keep going step by step until you reach the summit. The only way to get to the top is to start! You won't be able to reach financial freedom if you keep procrastinating. Once you have taken your first few steps, let me know how you are doing and we can compare notes. Perhaps we can teach each other some lessons that can be shared with the world.

FURTHER READING

Brinson, Gary P., L. Randolph Hood and Gilbert Beebower. 'Determinants of portfolio performance', *Financial Analysts Journal* 42(4), July–August 1986, pp. 39–44.

Brown, Brené. *Daring Greatly: How the Courage to Be Vulnerable Transforms the Way We Live, Love, Parent, and Lead.* Penguin Life, 2012.

Clason, George Samuel. *The Richest Man in Babylon.* Penguin Books, 1926.

Dimson, Elroy, Paul Marsh and Mike Staunton. *Credit Suisse Global Investment Returns Yearbook 2017.* Credit Suisse Research Institute, 2017.

Eichholtz, Piet M.A. 'A Long Run House Price Index: The Herengracht Index, 1628–1973', University of Maastricht–Limburg Institute of Financial Economics (LIFE), 1994.

Gladwell, Malcolm. *Outliers: The Story of Success.* New York: Little, Brown and Company, 2008.

Harari, Yuval Noah. *Homo Deus: A Brief History of Tomorrow.* London: Harvill Secker, 2015.

Schroeder, Alice. *Snowball: Warren Buffett and the Business of Life.* London: Bloomsbury, 2009.

Sinek, Simon. *Start With Why.* New York: Portfolio, 2009.

Stanley, Thomas J. and William D. Danko. *The Millionaire Next Door: The Surprising Secrets of America's Wealthy.* New York: Pocket Books, 1998.

UBS. 'Life themes: Investing in volatile times', Part 1, *Many Ways to Rome: Comparing Different Investment Approaches*. June 2009.

Vanguard Group. 'Dollar cost averaging just means taking risk later', July 2012.

Vollset, Stein Emil, et al. 'Fertility, mortality, migration, and population scenarios for 195 countries and territories from 2017 to 2100: A forecasting analysis for the Global Burden of Disease Study', *The Lancet* 396(10258), 17 October 2020, pp. 1285–1306.

Zagorsky, Jay L. 'Marriage and divorce's impact on wealth', *Journal of Sociology* 41(4), 1 December 2005, pp. 406–424.

ABOUT THE AUTHOR

Warren Ingram is an award-winning financial planner and respected personal finance commentator. He has written two best-selling personal finance books, *Become Your Own Financial Advisor* and *How to Make Your First Million*. He is the co-founder of Galileo Capital and has been managing global investments for private investors for more than two decades. Warren hosts the *Honest Money* podcast and is a regular media commentator on personal finance and investment topics.